What Every
Virginia Woman
SHOULD KNOW
about
DIVORCE

second edition

Printed in the United States of America.
ISBN: 978-1-59571-321-6

Word Association Publishers
205 Fifth Avenue
Tarentum, PA 15084
www.wordassociation.com

What Every
Virginia Woman
SHOULD KNOW
about
DIVORCE

second edition

by
CHARLES R. HOFHEIMER, ESQ.
www.virginiadivorceattorney.com

WORD ASSOCIATION PUBLISHERS
TARENTUM, PENNSYLVANIA

INCLUDING

- 25 important truths for women confronting divorce
- 20 Guidelines for "separation under the same roof"
- 13 critical factors used to determine spousal support
- 3 types of property classification recognized by VIRGINIA courts
- 10 factors your judge must consider in a contested custody case
- the formula to determine your percentage share of his retirement benefits
- 38 Financial Records you should be aware of
- 20 steps to prepare for divorce
- 7 stages of divorce
- 40 age appropriate books about divorce for children

CONTENTS

Who is Behind This Book and Why Should I Listen
    to the Author?   1

25 Important Truths For Women
    Confronting Divorce   5

The Bare Basics   11

Who Should File First?   17

Pendente Lite   19

What Does the Process Actually Entail?   21

Divorce Complaint   24

What is the Underlying Reason for the Divorce?   28

How You Obtain Information After a Divorce is Filed   41

Spousal Support   58

The Cardinal Rules About Custody   72

Combined Support Worksheet   76

15 Questions to Consider Before Hiring
    Your Divorce Lawyer   79

Steps to Prepare for Divorce   87

Financial Records With Which Every Woman
    Should be Familiar   91

The High Cost of Divorce vs. the IRS   93

Resource List   95

Stages of Divorce   105

Children's Age Appropriate Books on Divorce   109

About the Author   115

WARNING AND DISCLAIMER

This book is in the nature of general information, not specific legal advice.

Please use this book for informational purposes only.

WHO IS BEHIND THIS BOOK

and

"WHY SHOULD I LISTEN TO THE AUTHOR"

Relax. Slow down. Breathe. It's going to be okay. The prospect of going through a divorce may seem daunting, but take a deep breath and begin the process one baby step at a time. I have seen women go through the process and come through stronger and sleeker, brightened and relieved of baggage while feeling more free and unencumbered.

If you are a woman contemplating or confronting divorce, you don't have to do it alone. Help, guidance and information to empower you is readily available. I want you to know:

1. The different and distinctive ways you can resolve your divorce.

2. That truly effective professionals abound in our community who can help you organize and structure your life into manageable parts so that your divorce does not seem so daunting and overwhelming.

3. That understanding the laws that govern divorce and understanding the process of di-

vorce helps relieve the stress of divorce. Knowledge is power!

My name is Charlie Hofheimer, and I have been a lawyer since 1972 and have been representing only women in divorce and custody cases since 1992. I started a law firm representing women only in divorce because I sensed a need to create a compassionate community of professionals to assist in educating and representing women as they navigate through the divorce process with a sense of confidence and a feeling of support.

With my wife, Diane Hofheimer, as my paralegal, we set out to change the dynamic of how women are represented and treated by their attorneys in the divorce process. We wanted to educate women about divorce, so we started a seminar program "What Women Need to Know About Divorce." This program has enlightened, buttressed and emboldened thousands of women from every imaginable background and profession.

Today, Diane, with whom I have been married for 42 years, and I work together with one of our daughters, Attorney Kristen Hofheimer. The other lawyer members of our firm are Jeffrey Tarkington, Sheera Herrell, Mary Elizabeth Davis and Shannon Lemm.

Our "legal family" of attorneys and staff recognize that women confronting divorce are facing a momentous time in their lives and are often caught between various confusing emotions and conflicting loyalties. If you are like most women, you are trying to make sense of the prospect of change - for you, your children, your extended family and your friends.

What this book offers you is not a panacea to all your problems, but it does provide you a wealth of information.

For more information, go to *www.virginiadivorceattorney.com* or *www.virginiacollaborativedivorceattorney.com*

For information about our monthly seminars "What Women Need to Know About Divorce" go to *www.monthlydivorceseminars.com*

25 IMPORTANT TRUTHS FOR WOMEN CONFRONTING DIVORCE

As we get started, I want to share some basic truths about divorce that I have learned while helping women get divorced.

1. Look out for yourself first! If you're okay, your kids will be okay. Just like on the airplane, you need to give yourself oxygen so you will be able to give it to them.

2. Never ever ever let him know you **FEAR** going to court! Embrace the court; it can be your best friend.

3. Turn his voice off in your head. He is no longer the authoritative figure in your life: you are.

4. Don't be predictable. In fact, do the unexpected; it throws him off balance. He will see he is dealing with someone new - a stronger, more focused, more autonomous you.

5. Don't sign anything!! (Unless your attorney says it's okay and you understand the ramifications).

6. When you negotiate, listen! Then take time to discuss with your "Board of Advisors." Listening is the key. Know what you are confronting. Listen to the nuances and underlying agenda.

7. When in doubt, do nothing. Then talk to a divorce professional (mental health provider, divorce financial professional or divorce lawyer).

8. When he says "Trust Me" - DON'T!!!

9. Fear - "False Expectation Appearing Real". Write out your worst case scenario and then write out how you will overcome it. Then the F.E.A.R. evaporates.

10. CHOOSE Wisely. You can CHOOSE to be the victim or you can CHOOSE to move on with your life. No one, and I mean no one, can make that choice for you.

11. Nobody will look out for you like you will. The best attorney in the world cannot know or care as much about your outcome as you do, so partner with your attorney, set achievable goals and keep communicating with your attorney.

12. Do not make your children your confidantes during your divorce – children should be allowed to remain children, no matter how you feel or what you think. Protect and love them like only a mother can.

13. Divorce is about outcome, not fault. See the big picture.

14. Custody is about CHILDREN, not fault. Use the term *"co-parenting"*, not *"custody"* or *"visitation"* when speaking with your husband.

15. The "Law" is not always fair; it is "The Law." It's not called the "Fairhouse." It's called the "Courthouse". Your attorney will help you benefit your case in this unfamiliar venue.

16. Be as thoughtful and visionary in planning your divorce as you did in planning your marriage.

17. Be observant and resourceful. Gather documents like tax returns, pension statements, bank accounts, and anything that helps document your financial situation.

18. Read the actual laws governing spousal support, child support, custody and property division (called "equitable distribution") for yourself.

19. Take down your "myspace," "yahoo singles" and other social networking pages. Make sure to print a copy of his internet pages or other signs of internet dalliances.

20. Get your own new e-mail account with a brand new password! Still, be careful what you send into cyberspace because most of this can be traced.

21. Never ever, ever move out and temporarily leave your children with their dad; it is a sure way to lose physical custody. Always do and be what best serves your children.

22. Don't move out with the children unless you have a detailed plan of action with your attorney and even then, understand that this may put you at risk of losing physical custody. This should only be done after careful consultation with an attorney who fully understands your situation.

23. If you do not have children, but need spousal support, don't leave home without a plan of action agreed to by you and your lawyer. Ask your attorney about the "ALS" rule. Virginia is a fault state and you need to understand what might put you at fault before making a move.

24. Be cognizant that the only limitation regarding the terms of a Separation Agreement is the creativity of its author.

25. Your Separation Agreement is your **Constitution**, your **Bill of Rights** and your **Declaration of Independence** all written up in one agreement. Make sure an experienced divorce attorney reviews it on your behalf *BEFORE YOU SIGN IT!*

Now that I have articulated some key points, I want to impart my PROMISE TO YOU!

> You are in the right place at the right time because we will empower you. You will have answers to more divorce questions than most women ask. And, odds are that you will not only know more than your husband, but that you will also know more about getting divorced than 99 percent of the men who inhabit this planet!

So, Let's get STARTED
THE BARE BASICS

How do I get him out of the house?

Of all the issues we will discuss, this is among the toughest to answer. Absent provable abuse entitling you to a Protective Order issued by a Juvenile and Domestic Relations District Court, you can't make him leave and most judges simply won't kick him out. Adjust accordingly for the time being.

You may ask, why can't I kick him out of the house? He is making life miserable for me and the kids!

Perhaps no issue is more vexing than when a family is headed for divorce and you want your husband out of the home. There are simply no easy answers to resolve this matter. The courts are very reluctant to forcefully remove anyone from his home unless there is very clear evidence of physical threat. The underlying reason for this goes back to the old English common law that your home is your castle and the king was unable to enter your home absent a writ from the court. Again, adjust accordingly, with the long-term picture in mind. Keep in mind, your husband may be trying to get you to leave the marital home and you may need counsel as to whether you should leave and when and how you would leave. You do not want to leave without a jointly agreed upon strategy with your attorney.

Furthermore, you wonder, can we be separated while living in the same house?

To be "separated" means one of the parties has left the marriage and presumably the marital home with the intent not to return. Thus, the short answer to "Can we be separated while living in the same house?" is no. But there have been exceptions in the Virginia case law that leave open the door of possibility of an in-home separation. One must realize what the risk of such a separation entails before undertaking such an endeavor.

GUIDELINES FOR SEPARATION UNDER THE SAME ROOF

- Use separate bedrooms.
- Do not engage in romantic or sexual intimacy.
- Each spouse should shop for his or her own food, prepare his or her own meals; should not shop for the other, including clothing and other necessities.
- Do not use the other spouse's food or other purchases.
- Do not eat meals together (exceptions: holidays or children's birthdays).
- Each spouse should be responsible for caring for his or her own space within the home.
- Each spouse should do his or her own laundry.
- Use a separate and secure computer. Still, be careful what you use the computer for.
- Use a separate and secure telephone/cell phone for personal and business calls.
- Establish separate checking accounts.
- Cease socializing together, e.g., do not attend parties, movies, theater, etc. together.
- Do not attend church together.
- When there are minor children, interact as parents only where strictly necessary from the chil-

dren's perspective and their well-being, e.g., it would be acceptable for the parents to go together to a meeting with a school official relative to problems confronting a particular child, but less appropriate for the parents to ride together and sit together at a child's school play or soccer game.

- Cease gift giving between spouses for such occasions as birthdays, Christmas, anniversary, Valentine's Day, etc.

- Make known to close associates, relatives, etc. that you are not living as man and wife, but are separated within the residence.

- Have an objective third party come to the home from time to time to personally observe the two spouses' separate and distinct living quarters (bedrooms, bathrooms, etc.).

- Utilize separate entrances to the residence if feasible.

- Be prepared to explain reasons for living separately under the same roof, e.g., financial considerations; unavailability of separate residence; easing children's transition to parental separation, etc.

- Do not role play as the happy couple in front of neighbors and social acquaintances. You cannot "hold yourselves out" as husband and wife to the community.

WARNING: Living separately within the same residence as your spouse can be very difficult to prove to a judge. You may discover that the judge will not accept "your separate under the same roof" status and tell you to come back after a year of living separately in your own residences. This could pose an added expense as well as a delay to your divorce process.

The reason for this warning is that it is clear that the courts do not favor "living in the same residence" separations, and most judges will not award a divorce relying on an in-home separation; however, there are reported cases where judges have permitted separation under the same roof, provided that many, if not all, of the conditions indicated in the checklist are followed.

Presentation counts: confusing cohabitation, collusion and public policy

In Virginia, "cohabitation" is living together as if married. This does not mean that one has to be having sex with one's partner in order to be deemed a family in the eyes of the law. Accordingly, because a couple has not had intimacy for a while does not mean that the two aren't cohabiting. Thus, when you live together in a home, you are holding yourself out to the public essentially as a family, which is a contradiction of the element of "intent to separate." Oftentimes, couples do not want their friends to know that they are getting separated or divorced, and the Commonwealth of Virginia essentially is saying that if you intend to be separated or divorced, then you must present yourselves as being separated in order to obtain a divorce. You cannot appear to be married while claiming to be separated.

Furthermore, when you live together with your spouse, but claim you are separated, there is a great chance for "collusion" in the eyes of the court. Remember, it would be collusion if a husband and wife fraudulently claimed that they were separated, when in fact they were not. Finally, the public policy of the Commonwealth of Virginia is to support the family and marriage. Thus, the Commonwealth, through the legislature and the courts, wants to make it more, rather than less difficult to get divorced. Accordingly, the intent to separate is not readily manifested in an in-home separation.

GETTING THE DIVORCE STARTED
WHO SHOULD FILE FIRST?

I always encourage my clients to file first if they want temporary (*Pendente Lite*) support, custody, exclusive possession of the residence (pending the final divorce hearing) and other relief as spelled out in the motion for *pendente lite* relief (see pages 19-20) The reason for filing first is both strategic and tactical.

Doing so is **STRATEGIC** because often times husbands need a legal wake-up call to show that they are not in control anymore and to also let them know that you are leveling the playing field with your new lawyer.

Doing so is **TACTICAL** because when you file your Complaint for Divorce, you are also going to have him served a notice and motion for temporary (*Pendente Lite*) relief. When you file this *Pendente Lite* Motion first, you get to speak first. This means <u>your</u> lawyer, representing you, the "moving party", gets first dibs on influencing the judge with your view of the facts.

At the conclusion of the temporary support and custody hearing, your lawyer speaks, then your husband's lawyer speaks and then often your lawyer gets the benefit of the last word. While the last word is not always permitted in temporary hearings, it is always permitted in the final custody or divorce hearings, and it is a valuable right; the right of being the last to be heard when trying to influence the judge.

VIRGINIA: IN THE CIRCUIT COURT OF THE CITY OF VIRGINIA BEACH

JOAN A. SMITH,

    Plaintiff,

v.   CASE NO.: _____

WILLIAM R. SMITH,

    Defendant.

NOTICE

PLEASE TAKE NOTICE that on Friday, February 8, 2008 at 9:30 a.m., or as soon thereafter as counsel may be heard, the undersigned shall move this Honorable Court for entry of an order, pendente lite, awarding Plaintiff (Wife) custody of the child(ren) born of the marriage; support money for the support, maintenance and education of said child(ren); temporary and permanent spousal support for her support and maintenance; medical and hospitalization coverage for the Plaintiff (Wife) and child(ren); attorney's fees and costs associated herewith; an Order enjoining the Defendant (Husband) from disposing of any personal or marital assets from the estate to ensure that they will be available to meet any decree which may b ...ered in this suit; an Order enjoining the Defendant (Husband) from bothering, harassing or otherwise interfering with the Plaintiff (Wife) and restraining him from contacting her at home or at work, and from coming onto the premises where the Plaintiff (Wife) lives or works; that Defendant (Husband) be restrained from discussing the divorce around the child(ren) of the marriage; that the Defendant (Husband) have no unrelated overnight guests of the opposite sex when the child(ren) have overnight visitation with him and that the child(ren) have absolutely no contact with Defendant (Husband)'s paramours; that the Plaintiff (Wife) be awarded

exclusive use and possession of the marital residence so that she may reside there with the

child(ren) ; that Plaintiff (Wife) be awarded attorney fees pursuant to § 20-103 to go

forward with the suit both temporary and permanent, and Court costs; and for such further

and other relief as in equity may seem meet or the nature of her cause deems just.

JOAN A. SMITH

By_____
Of Counsel

Charles R. Hofheimer, Esquire
HOFHEIMER/FERREBEE, P.C.
1060 Laskin Road, Suite 12B
Virginia Beach, VA 23451
(757) 425-5200
(757) 425-6100 fax

OKAY -
LET THE DIVORCE BEGIN -
WHAT DOES THE PROCESS
ACTUALLY ENTAIL?

Assume for a moment that your spouse has left you a note saying "I am leaving and I'm not coming back!". In turn, you decide to file for divorce. Once you've made the decision to file for a divorce, normally you would hire an attorney and this person would file what is known as a Complaint (see Page 24-27). The Complaint contains certain facts like date of marriage, date of separation, names of children, birth dates of children, marriage location, the parties' residence location at the time of separation, and whether fault or no-fault grounds exist with regards to the divorce. You will normally sign the complaint under oath, or alternatively, your attorney may sign the complaint on your behalf. You are now known as the "Plaintiff." The Complaint is then filed in the circuit court for the city where you last lived as husband and wife, or alternatively, where your husband, now known as the "Defendant," currently resides.

After processing the Complaint, the Clerk of the Circuit Court will either forward it to the Sheriff's Office for service, or you may hire a private process server who will serve the Complaint on your husband. The current cost of filing a divorce in 2008 is $79.00 and the cost of service by the Sheriff's Office is $12.00, whereas the cost of service by a private process server will normally be between $20.00 and $50.00. The cost of private process service can be much higher if there are difficulties in serving your husband. The actual divorce doesn't really start until your husband is served with the Complaint.

If your husband has a girlfriend (or boyfriend), we will often use a private process server to serve your husband when he is with her to let him know we know! Sometimes, when we serve your husband, we will also serve "her" with a Notice of Deposition so she can put pressure on him to get the case settled. She may say to him: "Do not let me be cross-examined by your wife's lawyer!".

Within twenty-one days following the service of the Complaint on your husband, he will normally file an Answer and often a Cross-Complaint. His Answer usually denies your allegations against him. His Cross-Complaint will contain his allegations against you. It is not uncommon for answers or cross-complaints to have exaggerated allegations against you. More often than not, the allegations are designed to disturb you or intimidate you. Moreover, sometimes the allegations as written by your husband's attorney are as much to show his or her own client his lawyer is "tough" than it is about your actual conduct. Remember, the attorney is creatively writing what he or she was told and is trying to make it as negative as possible about you. Don't let it push your buttons; stay calm. Remember, do the unexpected, and do not let him shake you. Someone, either your husband or his attorney, is trying to get under your skin.

If issues of temporary support need to be immediately addressed, then a *Pendente Lite* hearing is scheduled, where the court will rule on temporary spousal and child support, temporary custody and visitation, hospitalization insurance and restraining orders regarding possession of the home, no harassment, no wasting of assets and if minor children are involved, no unrelated overnight guests of the opposite sex. Once these issues are addressed and ruled upon by the court, then the longer-term issues regarding your divorce can be addressed during the time remaining before your Final Divorce.

VIRGINIA: IN THE CIRCUIT COURT OF THE CITY OF VIRGINIA BEACH

JOAN A. SMITH,

      Plaintiff,

v.   CASE NO.: _____

WILLIAM R. SMITH,

      Defendant.

COMPLAINT

COMES NOW the Plaintiff, Joan A. Smith, by counsel, and for her complaint against the Defendant (Husband), states as follows to-wit:

1.   The parties are husband and wife having been lawfully married on June 20, 1995, in Virginia Beach, Virginia.

2.   There were two children born of the marriage, namely Rebecca L. Smith, born October 30, 1997, and Jason W. Smith, born April 19, 1999; there were no children born to either party and adopted by the other, nor adopted by the parties.

3.   The Plaintiff (Wife) is a resident and bona fide domiciliary of the Commonwealth of Virginia and has been for at least six months next preceding the filing of the suit for divorce.

4.   The Plaintiff (Wife) resides in the City of Virginia Beach and the Defendant (Husband) resides in the City of Virginia Beach.

5.   The parties last resided as husband and wife at 1245 Wolf Street in the City of Virginia Beach, Virginia.

6.   The Defendant (Husband) is a member of the Armed Forces of the United States.

7.   Both parties are of sound mind, over the age of 18 years, <u>sui juris</u> and neither party

1

is incarcerated in a mental or penal institution.

8.   On January 10, 2008, without just cause or provocation, the Defendant (Husband) deserted the Plaintiff (Wife) and the parties have been living separate and apart, uninterrupted and without marital cohabitation since that date and there is no likelihood of reconciliation.

9.   That since the separation of the parties, the Defendant (Husband) has continuously bothered, molested and harassed your Plaintiff (Wife) to the extent that your Plaintiff (Wife)'s and the children's health and well-being are being impaired.

10.   That the Defendant (Husband) has been guilty of cruelty toward the Plaintiff (Wife), causing reasonable apprehension of bodily harm in that the Defendant (Husband), over a period of many months physically abused, threatened, humiliated and degraded the Plaintiff (Wife) and subjected her to his violent and uncontrolled fits of temper, terrorizing the household; Defendant (Husband)'s conduct has completely deposed the Plaintiff (Wife) as a wife, rendered the marital state intolerable. Specifically on December 30, 2007, Defendant (Husband) pushed Plaintiff (Wife) up against a wall causing her to fall and on January 10, 2008 Defendant (Husband) threw a set of keys at Plaintiff (Wife) which struck her in her left arm leaving a bruise. Said conduct upon the part of the Defendant (Husband) is tantamount to constructive desertion, and the parties have been separated continuously since that time without interruption and without cohabitation and there is no likelihood of reconciliation.

11..   That on diverse dates and locations including, but not limited to, December 29, 2007 and January 10, 2008 in Virginia Beach, Virginia, Defendant (Husband) has been guilty of adultery and/or sodomy with a person not your Plaintiff (Wife), whose name is Elaine B. Rushing, said adultery having taken place at the Notel Hotel located on Paramour Lane in

2

Virginia Beach, Virginia. This adultery and/or sodomy has taken place within the past five years without the knowledge, consent or connivance of your Plaintiff (Wife), and the parties have lived separate and apart since January 10th, 2008 and that there is no likelihood of reconciliation.

WHEREFORE, and for as much as your Plaintiff (Wife) is remediless, save in a Court of Equity, your Plaintiff (Wife) prays that the said Defendant (Husband) be made a party to these proceedings; that all proper process may be issued; that a divorce, A MENSA ET THORO, pursuant to §20-95 of the Code of Virginia, 1950, as amended, be decreed your Plaintiff (Wife), to be later merged into a divorce A VINCULO MATRIMONII at the expiration of one year's separation on the grounds of desertion and cruelty pursuant to § 20-91(6) and adultery pursuant to §20-91(1) of the Code of Virginia, 1950, as amended; or, in the alternative, that a divorce A VINCULO MATRIMONII be decreed your Plaintiff (Wife) on the grounds of a one year separation pursuant to § 20-91(A)(9)(a) of the Code of Virginia, 1950, as amended; that the Plaintiff (Wife) be awarded attorney fees pursuant to § 20-103 to go forward with the suit both temporary and permanent, and Court costs; that the Plaintiff (Wife) be awarded custody of the children born of the marriage of the parties; that the Plaintiff (Wife) be awarded support money for the support, maintenance and education of said children; that the Plaintiff (Wife) be awarded temporary and permanent spousal support or a reservation of right; that the Defendant (Husband) be denied spousal support: that the Defendant (Husband) be required to maintain health and major medical insurance on the Plaintiff (Wife) and children; the Plaintiff (Wife) seeks an injunction against the Defendant (Husband) from bothering and harassing and otherwise interfering with the Plaintiff (Wife); that the Defendant (Husband) be restrained from contacting the Plaintiff (Wife) at home or at work, and from coming onto the premises where the Plaintiff

3

(Wife) lives or works; that the Defendant (Husband) be restrained from discussing the divorce around the children of the marriage, and that he have no unrelated overnight guests of the opposite sex when the children have overnight visitation with him; the Plaintiff (Wife) seeks "equitable distribution" of the "marital property", monetary award, civilian or military retainer, and any other retirement pension, if any, pursuant to § 20-107.3 of the Code of Virginia and allocation of marital debt; for an injunction against the Defendant (Husband) requiring that he preserve his estate so that it will be forthcoming to meet any Decree which may be made in this suit, including an injunction enjoining and restraining him from disposing of any property, marital or otherwise, without court order; that the Plaintiff (Wife) be awarded exclusive use and possession of the marital residence so that she may reside there with the children; and that the Plaintiff (Wife) have such further and other relief in the premises as the nature of her cause may require or the Court in equity may deem meet and proper.

_____
Joan A. Smith

STATE OF VIRGINIA
CITY OF VIRGINIA BEACH, to-wit:

    Before me, the undersigned Notary Public in and for the aforesaid City and State, personally appeared Joan A. Smith, who, after first being placed under oath, swore that the allegations contained in the foregoing Complaint are true to the best of her knowledge this _____ day of _____, 2008.

_____
Notary Public

My commission expires:_____

4

Of Counsel

Charles R. Hofheimer, Esquire
HOFHEIMER/FERREBEE, P.C.
Sandpiper Key
1060 Laskin Road, Suite 12B
Virginia Beach, Virginia 23451
[757] 425-5200 phone [757] 425-6100 fax

5

GROUNDS FOR DIVORCE - WHAT IS THE UNDERLYING REASON FOR THE DIVORCE?

One of the questions I'm frequently asked is, "What are the grounds for divorce in Virginia?" You may know what your grounds are, but what legitimates a divorce in a court of law? The grounds for divorce are adultery, sodomy, buggery, felony conviction, cruelty, apprehension of bodily hurt, desertion, abandonment and one year of separation (no-fault).

ADULTERY, SODOMY AND BUGGERY

The fault grounds based on sexual misconduct: 1)Adultery—sexual intercourse; 2) Sodomy—oral or anal sex and 3)Buggery—sex with animals, are difficult grounds to prove in Virginia. Adultery and sodomy are defined as any married person voluntarily having sexual intercourse, oral sex, or anal sex with any person who is not his or her spouse. The problem in Virginia is that the proof must be strict, satisfactory and conclusive. Testimony or admissions must be corroborated. This means there must be some definitive evidence beyond the mere suspicions or admissions by your husband that he had an affair.

Oftentimes, if your husband's girlfriend (we will call her "Ms. Feckless") was subsequently jilted by your husband, she may be willing to testify against him. If Ms. Feckless will speak to you or your attorney, she may give you detailed facts and information that will help you prove your case and may often help catch your husband lying in court. She can give you the location where they met (The No-tell Motel), the dates and times of day, what each was wearing-lots of information that implies that either you had a private investigator present or that she is "spilling the beans."

If you are not fortunate enough to have Ms. Feckless in an alliance with you, then the effort to prove adultery becomes more difficult.

To prove adultery, you must prove a sexual relationship. Obviously, 99.9% of the time this is impossible to do by picture, video, audio, or communication tracking (putting a GPS responder on a car). More often than not, adultery is proven in stages—you first find out that something is going on with your husband, (i.e.) changes in his lifestyle, sexual habits, text messaging, surprising e-mails, or cell phone irregularities—something that raises your level of vigilance. Often, either you or your private investigator begin putting facts together. I have had many clients work with their friends to observe their husband meeting someone. For verification purposes, always take one or two friends with you who can serve as witnesses to the same things you observed. Also, use rental cars so license plates can't be traced.

There is nothing wrong with doing some initial "investigating" on your own, but be aware it is difficult to unobtrusively follow someone. Before you do so, know that once your cover is blown, the chances of gathering future proof dwindle significantly. You may also be accused of stalking. Think this through before taking rash actions.

Let's say you have a picture of Ms. Feckless kissing or holding hands with your husband, and you have found a Hallmark card from her to him saying "I Love You" and "Can't wait to be with you." Despite this, you still lack sufficient legal evidence.

So, the next night you drive by Ms. Feckless' house at 11:00 p.m., and there is your husband's car, parked in the driveway. Of course, after returning home, you can't sleep at all, so you drive by the house at 4:00 a.m. and every hour thereafter. The car hasn't moved. When you return at 7:00 a.m., the car is gone, but, you have pictures of the car at her house at 11:00 p.m., 4:00 a.m., 5:00 a.m., and 6:00 a.m. This still does not prove adultery in court. Why? It could be argued that someone else drove the car, (i.e. Ms. Feckless' car broke down; he lent her his, and he slept at the office). While this is unlikely, the law considers this possibility.

A week later you employ a private investigator who video tapes the pair walking on the beach, hand in hand. This investigator observes both of them entering her home. The investigator stays all night, observing both entrances to ensure that no one can say they left an hour later by way of the back door. The investigator sees all the lights go out in the house, and records your soon-to-be ex opening the front door in his "shorts" to retrieve the newspaper. One and a half hours later, he again opens the door dressed in his suit and kisses Ms. Feckless and walks to his car. BINGO! You probably have proved your case! But remember, "clear and convincing" evidence is a tougher legal standard than "preponderance of the evidence," so some judges still may say the case is insufficiently proven. The courts can be difficult to navigate, so being armed with this awareness of your hefty "burden of proof" is essential. You need to know what you are up against but not lose sight of your reasons for your divorce. You may be fighting for your life–your right to live freely and independently, your right to own and direct your journey. What you are fighting for is precious–don't be discouraged. Sharpen your strategy, using your attorney as your ally.

**Another important word here: Before employing a private investigator, ask for referrals from a lawyer. Some investigators may be good investigators but lousy in court under cross-examination. You need one who is good at both.

Another important point is that one error often made by attorneys when pleading adultery is failing to plead sodomy. I had a client who performed oral sex on her boyfriend but did not have intercourse because in her mind she was married and intercourse was sacred, only to be experienced with her husband. His attorney alleged she committed adultery, which she could honestly deny. But this still raised red flags. It taught me the importance of including the sodomy allegation if you are alleging adultery as you seldom, if ever, really know what takes place behind closed doors.

Now is the appropriate time to issue an **IMPORTANT WARNING**; If your husband has had an affair, and you engage in sex with him after learning of the marital infidelity, then you have condoned the act, meaning you have forgiven him in the eyes of the law. Do not let this happen; too much is at stake.

And here is a **DOUBLE WARNING**: Adultery can have a substantial impact on your ability to plead your case and have your case legitimated. In stark simple terms, adultery can have an economic impact affecting you and your children, if you have children.

If a wife is guilty of adultery or sodomy committed outside of the marriage and it can be proven sufficiently to be a grounds of divorce, then the Court *shall not award permanent* (note, not temporary) maintenance or spousal support!!! Do not venture into this risky territory. There is too much to lose. (If you committed adultery, never admit to it to anyone unless and until you talk to your lawyer.) Also, know there is a five year statute of limitations, so an affair older than five years should be of no legal consequence.

Manifest Injustice-Notwithstanding the denial of spousal support because the proposed recipient committed adultery or sodomy, there is an exception that "if the court determines by clear and convincing evidence that a denial of support or maintenance would constitute a manifest injustice, based on the respective degrees or fault during the marriage and the relative economic circumstances of the parties, the court can nonetheless make a spousal support award to the spouse committing adultery."

Adultery by either party is often taken seriously by the courts. It means there need be no waiting period to get divorced.

In fact, Adultery, Sodomy, and Buggery are the only fault grounds that don't require you to wait a specific period of time before you can obtain a divorce. In other words, if you can prove any of these was committed by your husband, you can get a divorce as soon as the case is prepared and you go to trial. There is no six month or one year waiting period.

FELONY CONVICTION

Divorce due to felony conviction requires that a spouse be convicted of a felony and sentenced to serve *more* than one year in jail in order for the innocent spouse to obtain a divorce based on the felony conviction.

DESERTION

Desertion requires that a party leave the marital home with the *intent* not to return. The intent may be proven by actions, words or conduct.

Often times, I advise clients who need to leave the marital residence for a short period of time to write a note to their spouse saying something along the lines of "I am going to my mother's, but I shall return in two weeks." If you write such a note, keep a copy of it, as oftentimes your spouse will say that he did not receive it. It is important that you in fact return to the marital residence, or you could be found guilty of desertion.

I have frequently had occasions where the husband has left the marital home; he then meets with an attorney and finds out he is guilty of desertion and moves back into the home. If you have not filed for divorce before he returns, you are probably stuck with him in the home until you work out a settlement. Obviously, this creates great stress on the family, as the courts are very reluctant to force anyone to leave his home absent family abuse. So, if your husband leaves, and you believe divorce is inevitable, file a Complaint for divorce immediately.

CONSTRUCTIVE DESERTION

Constructive Desertion is when the actions of your spouse are so inimical to the welfare of your family that you are in essence forced to leave the marital residence of your safety and well being. Do not seek the benefit of this reason for divorce without having legal advice.

CRUELTY OR REASONABLE APPREHENSION OF BODILY HURT.

Cruelty includes either physical acts or successive acts of ill treatment or bodily harm. The courts will distinguish between normal conduct of unhappy people and cruel conduct on the part of one of the spouses. Because of the available option to the court to declare a "no-fault divorce based on a one year separation," you see many cases filed on cruelty, but few divorces are actually granted on the grounds of cruelty. More often than not, the court or the parties will opt out for a "one year separation" divorce.

NO-FAULT

The final ground for divorce in Virginia is no-fault. If a couple has no minor children under the age of eighteen and they have entered into a written separation agreement, then they may obtain a divorce six months following their initial separation. If there are minor children, or if there is no written agreement, then the parties must wait one year before they may obtain a no-fault divorce. A no-fault divorce essentially eliminates the need to prove fault in order to obtain a divorce. If a year has passed, and you do not have a separation agreement, you must have a trial and provide evidence for why you should receive spousal support, evidence of your interest in property, evidence for child custody and for pension funds; you just don't have to prove fault.

FAULT OR NO-FAULT?

You may ask yourself the following question at this point: Why does it matter whether I have a fault divorce or a no-fault divorce? The answer is that it can matter a great deal. In a no-fault divorce, you cannot file a divorce complaint until six months have passed (if you have signed an agreement), or one year without an agreement. During this waiting period (before you file a bill of complaint) you can only file for custody, visitation, child support and/or spousal support in the Juvenile and Domestic Relations District Court. In many jurisdictions, you cannot schedule a hearing until six to eight weeks after you file your petition. Thus, if you do not have adequate finances, you may be in financial trouble while waiting to get into court. Plus, if you have a hearing, your husband can file an appeal, causing more legal expense because the issues will be heard a second time in Circuit Court. If he is ordered to pay you support in the Juvenile Court, your husband will also have to pay you support during the pendency of his appeal. Alternatively, he may file a divorce case the day before the Juvenile and Domestic Relations District Court hearing, further postponing your ability of obtaining custody and support.

On the other hand, if you have a fault divorce filed, then in most jurisdictions, you can get into court within two to three weeks. With a divorce, you file in the circuit court, a higher court than the domestic relations district court, and you can file for *pendente lite* relief. At a *pendente lite* hearing, unlike juvenile court, in addition to custody, visitation, child and spousal support, a circuit court can order exclusive possession of the residence to one of the parties as well as certain injunctions against dissipating assets, no haras ment, and certain prescriptions regarding conduct. Thus, with fault grounds you do not have a one-year limitation regarding the filing of the divorce, and normally it's easier to get into court to obtain financial support and other relief pending the outcome of the divorce.

AFFIRMATIVE DEFENSES

I do want to mention, though, that there are defenses to grounds for divorce. The five defenses are 1. *Condonation*: when the aggrieved spouse resumes cohabitation after learning of conduct constituting grounds for divorce. A good example would be that you find out that your spouse has committed adultery and you sleep with him after you become aware of his adulterous behavior. You have then legally condoned his unfaithful conduct. 2. *Insanity*: When the party at fault is insane. In order to be at fault, your husband has to have the mental capacity to understand his actions. 3. *Collusion*: when the parties make up a false ground for divorce. 4. *Recrimination*: when one of the parties commits adultery and the other spouse also has an affair to show the first offending spouse that she can have a paramour as well. In such a case, the court will grant neither of the parties divorce on the grounds of adultery. 5. *Connivance:* when one spouse agrees to the marital fault of the other and then alleges the fault as grounds to obtain a divorce. For instance, a wife cannot set up husband with a prostitute and then file divorce on adultery after he sleeps with her.

HOW YOU OBTAIN INFORMATION AFTER A DIVORCE IS FILED
THE DISCOVERY PROCESS

INTERROGATORIES

After the divorce has been filed, your husband will be asked by your attorney to answer questions regarding assets owned, debts owed, why he thinks he should have custody, et cetera. In Virginia, each of you may be asked to provide answers to "interrogatories" which normally are thirty or fewer questions requiring great detail about your assets, liabilities, fault, custody and such other issues as may be raised in the divorce. I have included five such questions just to give you an idea of the detail that is often requested.

1. *Provide the following information as to each employment position you have held during the past five years, whether full-time, part-time, or self-employment, free-lance or contract work, including but not limited to, your employer's name, the name of your immediate supervisor, each employer's full address and telephone number, your position, your dates of service,*

*your hours worked, your **current** monthly and annual gross income, **listing each source separately** (including bonuses, commissions, tips and overtime, stock options, deferred compensation for each year) and your fringe benefits (including insurance, retirement, profit sharing, travel pay, vacation and sick leave accrued), and state the reasons for any changes in employment and for your current employment state how often you are paid (i.e. monthly, every two weeks) and state the date when you are next paid.*

2. Provide the following information as to all bank accounts, in your name individually, jointly with any other person or in the name of any entity (i.e. partnership, corporation or otherwise) in which you have an interest, or that is held on your behalf, in any banking institutions, savings and loans, credit unions, stock brokerage firms, or other financial or financially related corporations, from January 1, 200___ to the date of your answers, stating the name, address and telephone number of the institution, each account number(s) and the type of account, owner(s) and signatories on each account, the balance of each account as of the date of separation, as well as the present balance(s) of the accounts.

3. *Provide the following information as to all Individual Retirement Accounts (IRA), Simplified Employee Pension Plans (SEP), Keogh Plans, profit-sharing, 401k plans, 403(B) plans, thrift savings plans, stock plans, retirement or pension plans, deferred compensation plans, defined contribution plans, defined benefits plan and annuities to which you are or may be entitled to receive benefits. State the name of the institution, where the funds are maintained, the business address and phone number of the institutional custodian of the funds, the name and account number of each account, the balance of each account as of separation, present balance, and whether you claim the funds are marital, separate, or hybrid.*

4. *If you believe that your spouse is not fit to have custody of or visitation with the child of the marriage, then state in detail what you allege to be the factors and circumstances which bring you to that conclusion including specific facts, actions, dates of occurrence, the persons involved and the persons witnessing such events.*

5. *Identify every person who has knowledge of the issues pending in this case, whether on the issue of the grounds of divorce, or on any financial issues such as custody, child support, spousal support or equitable distribution, stating their current address and their home and work phone*

numbers, their relationship to the parties involved; if the person will be called as an expert witness, state their name, address, telephone number, and profession, and set forth the subject matter on which the expert is expected to testify, the opinion they will express and a summary of the grounds for each opinion.

REQUEST FOR PRODUCTION OF DOCUMENTS

In addition to interrogatories, you're also permitted to ask for documents in your husband's possession or documents he has ready access to. This is called a "motion for production of documents" and again an example is provided.

Please Provide:

1. *All pay statements, or any other proof of income from any source, whether received from employers or from any entity in which you have an interest, reflecting gross income (whether taxable or non-taxable) and gains (realized or unrealized) and all withholdings, as well as income for overtime work, commissions, tips, bonuses, and all contracts and/or correspondence evidencing any terms or conditions of employment, that were in effect or were entered into, from January 1, 200___ to the present.*

2. *All savings, checking, depository, investment or
    loan account statements, checks, and registers,
    reflecting deposits, withdrawals, and account
    balances in any banking institutions, savings and
    loan association, credit union, brokerage ac-
    counts or accounts with other financial institu-
    tions or corporations, partnerships or businesses,
    whether such account has been held by you in-
    dividually, jointly with any other person, or in
    the name of any entity in which you have an in-
    terest, or that is held on your behalf, from Jan-
    uary 1, 200___ to the present.*

3. *All summary plan descriptions and/or state-
    ments for each pension or retirement benefits
    plan, expense account, cafeteria plan, profit-
    sharing, stock option plan, 401k plan, 403(b)
    plan, thrift savings plan, deferred compensation
    plan, IRA, Keogh, SEP, or other retirement or
    pension plan, vested or non-vested, as well as
    any military pension plans, either by reason of
    employment with another or from any entity in
    which you have an interest from January 1,
    200___ to the present.*

4. *All reports of any experts that you intend to call
    to testify at trial.*

5. *Any and all tangible evidence, including docu-
    ments, correspondence, letters, video and/or
    audio tape recordings, photographs or prepared*

exhibits which prove, support or are relevant to your petition for custody.

SUBPOENA DUCES TECUM

If your husband claims he has disposed of all of his statements, then the "stealth bomb" of discovery is used. This is a Subpoena Duces Tecum, which is a request to a third party to provide information. For example we can send a Subpoena Duces Tecum to your husband's employer requesting documents that will provide information about his benefits and retirement as well as copies of his last twelve months' pay records. While having to send a Subpoena Duces Tecum is an added expense, quite frequently it is very helpful in putting together accurate financial information.

ADMISSIONS

Another effective weapon in the discovery arsenal is a Request for Admissions. Admissions are very fact-specific and must be answered within 21 days. If you are ever served admissions and you fail to admit or deny an allegation, the allegation will be deemed admitted. Oftentimes, admissions are used to verify documents or other facts. Some Admissions examples follow:

- *Admit or deny that your total gross income for the year 2007 is $67,290.00.*

- *Admit or deny that you had a checking account at Bank of America with Ms. Feckless during the month of March of 2007.*

- *Admit or deny that you have contributed to a 401K Plan with your current employer during the calendar year 2007*

DEPOSITIONS

An expensive and less frequently used but very effective discovery process involves depositions. In a deposition, your husband is asked to appear with his attorney in your attorney's office and answer questions under oath before a court reporter and you. Depositions allow your attorney to ask your husband questions to gather further information and to lock in his testimony. Depositions are under oath and may be admitted as evidence in a court hearing, if the underlying questions are admissible. Depositions may also be taken of third parties such as girlfriends, babysitters, teachers or other persons who may have information important to your case. Frequently, successful depositions can expedite settlement.

MOTION TO COMPEL

What happens if your husband does not answer certain interrogatories or requests for production of documents or other such discovery requests? Your attorney then files a motion to compel asking the court to order him to appropriately answer the questions presented. His failure to do so after being ordered by the court could lead to a contempt hearing or the exclusion of specific evidence at trial. Such conduct is, also considered at the end of the case when attorney's fees are awarded.

OPTIONS TO RESOLVE YOUR DIVORCE CASE

After all the discovery information is obtained, there remain three options to resolve your divorce case. One option is to prepare a separation agreement containing terms that you wish to offer to your husband. The second option is to enter into mediation where you and your husband try to negotiate an agreement in the presence of a trained mediator. The third option is litigation, where you go into court, have a trial, and a judge rules on the outcome of your divorce. It is possible to actually engage in all three options or any one or two of them before your case is settled or tried.

SEPARATION AGREEMENT

Let's begin with the separation agreement. This is a document which records the resolution of financial issues, custody issues and any other matters that require resolution. Typically 90 to 95 percent of all divorces ultimately conclude with a separation agreement; however, how one arrives at resolution is often a convoluted process. The Separation Agreement is often the result of negotiations, mediation, collaboration, and sometimes, litigation.

In describing these resolution options, I have purposely left out the collaborative divorce model, as that will be covered in a separate section. The reason collaboration is not included is that one does not normally file a divorce complaint in a collaborative case, but rather, one agrees not to go to court and not to file a divorce suit until the matter is totally resolved with a written agreement.

NEGOTIATION

Turning to the option of negotiation of a separation agreement, it is common that negotiations commence with one side providing the other side a written offer of the terms by which they would settle the divorce. Then the other side responds with their terms of settlement. From here, the parties continue to give and take until all of the issues of the family are resolved. Remember, in negotiations, ultimatums are not looked upon favorably, as they make settlement of issues very difficult, if not impossible.

If the parties are able to amicably resolve matters through negotiations, then the end product will be a separation agreement which outlines all the terms of settlement. This document will then become the final terms of your divorce and will constitute much of your Final Decree of Divorce.

This brings to mind a *cardinal rule* that during a divorce a woman should never sign any documents without first having them reviewed by her attorney. Frequently, I have had women come to see me with an agreement they signed saying, "Oh, my husband told me this was just a temporary agreement" when, in fact, the document states right on the face of it that this is a final stipulation agreement. *I LIKEN THE IMPORTANCE OF A SEPARATION AGREEMENT TO YOUR BILL OF RIGHTS, YOUR CONSTITUTION AND YOUR DECLARATION OF INDEPENDENCE ALL ROLLED UP IN ONE DOCUMENT!* Accordingly, it is very important that you not sign any such document until your attorney has approved it. I cannot stress how many times women have brought signed agreements to me thinking that they could change the terms at a later time. They then become very disappointed when they find out that they are stuck with the terms of a less-than-favorable agreement. The courts of the Commonwealth of Virginia do not often set aside contracts, and the fact that a wife was emotionally depressed and/or incapable of saying "no" to her husband is seldom, if ever, sufficient grounds to legally undo a signed written agreement.

RULES ABOUT SEPARATION AGREEMENTS

First–The only limitation on the terms of your Separation Agreement is the creativity of its authors. There is no legal limit to the creativity encouraged in providing solutions to complicated issues. Don't ever let an attorney tell you there is only one way to create a favorable outcome. The options are as varied as you and your attorney's abilities to envision.

Second–A Separation Agreement is a *private* contract between you and your husband. **DO NOT WRITE AND SIGN YOUR OWN SEPARATION AGREEMENT WITHOUT HAVING IT REVIEWED BY AN EXPERIENCED DIVORCE ATTORNEY LOOKING OUT SOLELY FOR YOUR LEGAL INTERESTS. YOUR HUSBAND'S ATTORNEY CANNOT REPRESENT YOU!**

Third–Custody, Visitation and Child Support are always subject to change, so don't give away support or assets to obtain custody of your children. I have seen cases where the woman gave up financial assets for custody, only to lose custody several years later because her finances were unstable, while her former spouse was prospering financially. The pre-teen and teen kids wanted to live at the house with the pool, the big allowance, the ski vacations and the 4-wheeler and the *Guardian Ad Litem* (an attorney often appointed by the court to represent the child) disapproved of mom taking the youngest to work with her because she could not afford daycare. Do not let such a scenario happen to you.

In short, if you give up everything to obtain custody, you may well lose custody several years later, primarily because you gave up everything!

Fourth–In your Agreement, make sure you include times and dates when things are going to be completed. *Time is of the essence* may be the most important five words you use with regard to financial payments.

Fifth–Details are very important and add clarity. Be careful of broad strokes! Vagueness may create huge misunderstandings which can be exploited by your ex and expensive to resolve.

MEDIATION

A second method of resolving the terms of a divorce is mediation. Mediation is a process where you and your husband meet with one or more mediators to discuss and ultimately resolve the issues of your divorce. If the parties agree, they may bring their attorneys to their mediation sessions. My advice to women who choose the mediation process is to meet with their attorney in advance and develop an outline of the issues and an acceptable range of terms of agreement with regard to each issue. Going into mediation unprepared can be very costly. Furthermore, if a woman is intimidated by her spouse or does not feel that she has sufficient knowledge of the family assets and liabilities, then she needs to meet with her attorney and decide whether the mediation process can ultimately be entered into after she is educated about the assets and liabilities that her family possesses.

LITIGATION

The least favorable and most expensive process for getting divorced is the litigation model (i.e. fighting it out in court). Oftentimes, a woman may be forced into the litigation process against her will because her spouse will not resolve issues fairly. When this occurs, you will have a trial before a judge (no jury) where evidence will be presented on your behalf and on behalf of your husband. The judge will ultimately make decisions regarding each and every issue presented to him or her, and the final decree of divorce will be entered based on the judge's decision. The most important thing about litigation is to make sure that you and your attorney are fully prepared for the process. There are many strict deadlines for providing information to each of the parties and to the court which, if not followed, can be disastrous to your case. Accordingly, if you anticipate litigation, then you will need to be able to provide the time to become adequately prepared.

APPEAL

After your trial, the attorneys will draft a final decree of divorce based on the Court's decision, and it will be entered by the court. You will then have thirty days from the date of the entry of that order to note an appeal if you are dissatisfied with the outcome and you have legal or factual grounds upon which to base an appeal. The appellate process in Virginia usually takes between six months and a year and can be quite costly. Additionally, appellate courts do not readily overturn decisions of the Circuit Courts and you must have sound legal grounds for your appeal.

COLLABORATION

The collaborative divorce process is very new and permits couples to work through issues involving their children, their financial future and their property using joint problem solving techniques **without going to court**. With the help of supportive professionals serving in the capacity of coaches, child specialists and financial specialists, the clients, their attorneys, and all the other professionals, work together to achieve an agreement that addresses the interests and priorities of both spouses as well as the family as a whole. For more information about collaborative divorce, go to
www.collaborativepractice.com.
or www.virginiacollaborativelaw.com

ISSUES AND ENTITLEMENTS

When prospective clients come to see me, they want to know what they are entitled to and what they will receive. In order to provide this information, it is necessary to know many facts. Among them are the reasons for the divorce, the number of years of marriage, the number of children and their ages, what real-estate is owned, how and when was it acquired, what kind of life and health insurance they own and what are the assets of value and debts. Also requested is a narrative regarding each parent's contribution to the marriage, each parent's role in raising the children, and the relative incomes of the parties. For a non-working spouse, the court will be interested in the non-monetary contributions of the parties to the marriage. A checklist of non-monetary contributions follows. With this information, a beginning framework of entitlements may be explained.

NON-MONETARY CONTRIBUTIONS TO THE FAMILY

	ITEM	*W%*	*H%*	*COMMENTS*
1.	Food Purchaser			
2.	Cook/Chef			
3.	Meal Planning			
4.	Dishwasher			
5.	Maintenance-Inside			
6.	Maintenance-Outside			
7.	Cleaning			
8.	Laundry			
9.	Gardening			
10.	Lawn Care			
11.	Repairs-Inside			
12.	Repairs-Outside			
13.	Clothes Repair			
14.	Garbage Disposal			
15.	Pet Custodian			
16.	Errand Runner			
17.	Vacation/Move Planner			
18.	Bookkeeper/Budgeting			
19.	Merchandise Buyer			

CONT.

	ITEM	W%	H%	COMMENTS
20.	Gift Cards			
21.	Career Advisor			
22.	Promoting Career			
13.	Family Councelor			
14.	Religious Guidance			
25.	Infant Care			
16.	Child Care			
27.	Child Psychologist			
28.	Chauffeur			
29.	School Activities			
30.	Extra Curricular			
31.	Professor/Homework			
32.	Bedtime/Morning			
33.	Other			
Overall Contributions%				

SPOUSAL SUPPORT

In Virginia, there are four types of spousal support awards available in divorce. The courts are empowered to award any one type of support or any combination of types of support it deems appropriate. The types of support are: lump sum award, periodic payments, rehabilitive support for a fixed period of time, and reservation of right to ask for support at a future time. In determining the appropriateness of spousal support in a final divorce hearing, there are thirteen factors outlined in the spousal support section of the Virginia Code 20-107.1 (see below). It is helpful to go through each of the factors and write out your response to each for your attorney so that any unusual facts can be brought to his or her attention.

The Court **must** consider the following factors to determine spousal support.

FACTORS:

1. *The obligations, needs and financial resources of the parties, including but not limited to income from all pension, profit sharing or retirement plans, of whatever nature;*

2. *The standard of living established during the marriage; *Note - this does not mean that you are entitled to be in maintained in the lifestyle to which you become accustomed during the marriage. The reality is that the income that sup-*

ported the marital household cannot now support two households at the same level you and
your husband will both have to tighten your
belts a little. However it is far better to live happily with fewer luxuries than miserably with
800 cable TV channels.

3. The duration of the marriage;

4. The age and physical and mental condition of
the parties and any special circumstances of the
family;

5. The extent to which the age, physical or mental
condition or special circumstances of any child
of the parties would make it appropriate that a
party not seek employment outside of the
home;

6. The contributions, monetary and nonmonetary,
of each party to the well-being of the family;

7. The property interests of the parties, both real
and personal, tangible and intangible;

8. The provisions made with regard to the marital
property under §§ 20-107.3;

9. The earning capacity, including the skills, education and training of the parties and the present
employment opportunities for persons possess-
ing such earning capacity;

10. The opportunity for, ability of, and the time and
costs involved for a party to acquire the appropriate education, training and employment to

obtain the skills needed to enhance his or her earning ability;

11. *The decisions regarding employment, career, economics, education and parenting arrangements made by the parties during the marriage and their effect on present and future earning potential, including the length of time one or both of the parties have been absent from the job market;*

12. *The extent to which either party has contributed to the attainment of education, training, career position or profession of the other party; and*

13. *Such other factors, including the tax consequences to each party, as are necessary to consider the equities between the parties.*

One of the standard questions I receive during our "What Women Need to Know About Divorce" seminars is how long a woman is entitled to receive support if qualified for it. While there are no absolute rules nor presumptions in Virginia, a rule of thumb is helpful. If you have been married five years or fewer, it is possible that you may not be awarded any support, or you may be awarded limited support to last no longer than the length of your marriage. An award of support for a short marriage still requires the Court to look at all of the factors as enumerated above, but the Court is usually reluctant to burden a husband with long term spousal support for a short marriage. The award of support in a short marriage would also require that there be a significant disparity of income between you and your spouse.

On the other hand, if you have been married between six and twenty years and qualify for support, it would be reasonable to expect that you would be entitled to support for at least half the length of your marriage or longer, provided the Court finds that the appropriate factors exist: you are not at fault in causing the divorce, and there is an appropriate disparity of income between you and your husband. With a marriage longer than twenty years, absent fault on your part and assuming a disparity of income, one could realistically expect support until death of either party, remarriage of the receiving spouse or clear and convincing evidence of cohabitation with another in a relationship analogous to marriage for twelve months or longer.

Once it has been determined that you are entitled to support, the next obvious question is "How much support will I receive?" Unlike child support, there is no statewide formula for support awarded by final divorce decree; however, there are formulas used by various Courts for temporary support. If you are seeking support in the Juvenile Courts, then the Fairfax Guidelines are appropriate. The formula for the Fairfax guidelines is as follows:

A. *Payor 's Income x 28%*
B. *Payee's Income x 58%*
C. *Line A minus Line B equals proposed Spousal Support*

Courts around the Commonwealth have determined their own formulas for temporary (*pendente lite*) support hearings in divorce, and there are formulas in Fairfax, Richmond, and Harrisonburg. Generally, a look at the Fairfax Guideline is helpful in providing a client a range of spousal support she can expect. However, those guidelines are not binding on the court, and the issue of spousal support is left to the discretion of the judges.

The goals of the Court are different at a temporary support hearing early in the divorce versus the awarding of support in the final divorce decree. Early on in a *pendente lite* hearing where the Court has a very limited period of time to hear support witnesses and determine support, the Court's goal is to keep the situation relatively simple and to make an award either by formula like the Fairfax Guidelines, or based on the income of the parties and their expenses. Because *pendente lite* support has to be determined in a relatively short period of time, it is generally a function of weighing the income of the parties against the relative expenses. There was a move afoot in the Commonwealth to try and resolve *pendente lite* support by formula in order that people may have an idea of what they are entitled to with some consistency. Thus, in 2007, the legislature passed legislation applying the Fairfax Guidelines to Juvenile Court spousal support awards, but there is no statewide formula for spousal support in the Circuit Courts.

EQUITABLE DISTRIBUTION

How Virginia divides marital property (which includes all material possessions acquired by the parties during the marriage that are not separate property) between spouses is determined by Section 20-107.3 of the Code of Virginia. There are three basic types of property in Virginia: separate property, marital property and hybrid property. The definitions of these three types of property are very important, and your understanding of them is critical to your understanding of what you may or may not be entitled to in your divorce.

In your court case, it is up to the attorneys to identify all of the property of the marriage and then assist the Court with evidence to show whether the property is separate, hybrid or marital. The Court assumes that all property acquired during the marriage is marital, unless proven otherwise by one of the parties. The legal definitions of the types of property are as follows:

Separate property: This includes any property owned by one spouse prior to the marriage or after separation, or property acquired during the marriage by gift or inheritance from other than your spouse. Thus, if you had an antique chair that was passed on to you by the death of a family member, that would legally be your chair. Likewise, if your husband inherited $100,000.00 and kept it separate in an account and it is now worth $400,000.00, those are his separate funds.

Marital property: This includes all property, not otherwise separate, acquired during the marriage regardless of the name on the title. This means that if your husband bought a boat in his name during the marriage, with funds earned during the marriage, the boat is a marital asset, even though it may be legally titled only in his name. Likewise, the gold bracelet that your husband gave you for Christmas as a gift is a marital asset, notwithstanding the fact that it was a gift from him to you. The courts view a marriage as an economic partnership, and all monetary and non-monetary benefits of the husband and wife should be shared by the parties equitably but not necessarily equally.

Hybrid property: Property that is part separate and part marital. An example of this might be that your grandmother left you some money prior to your getting married, which you kept in a separate account. When buying your first house, you took that money, along with money that you and your husband had saved during the marriage, and you deposited your inheritance into the joint checking account and then a week later you two went to closing and paid for the home. In Virginia, if you can trace the origin of the funds and show where they came from and how they were applied, then that is known as a hybrid property because part came from separate funds and part came from marital funds. There are several ways to determine what percentage of the residence is your separate property and what percentage of the residence is jointly held marital property. How the physical property is titled may not be as important as how the house was funded, unless there was a Deed of Gift from one spouse to both spouses or solely to the other spouse, in which case the Deed of Gift will probably be applied.

Once all the assets and debts of the marriage are identified and the nature of their identity is determined, then it may be necessary to value the assets for the purpose of equitable distribution. Different assets are valued in different ways. For instance, a car would be valued by its Blue Book value, whereas a home's value would normally be determined by an appraiser, or a couple may agree to use the city assessed value of the real-estate. With antiques, experts may be called in to determine their value, unless the parties agree on their worth. After the assets have been identified and they have been valued, then the Court will determine how those assets are to be distributed between the parties.

Perhaps the most difficult evaluation issue arises from the ownership of a family business or a sole proprietorship. Evaluation experts are often required to value such assets, adding greatly to the expense of a divorce.

With real-estate assets, you are not only valuing the marital residence but you may well have to value vacation homes, timeshares, and/interests in rental homes.

The next class of assets is personal property like dishes, lamps, televisions, and furniture. Personal property must be identified and valued before distributed.

Usually we use an auctioneer to value everyday personal property.

With regard to personal property, the value is not what you paid for it but rather, what it is worth on the market today. For most people, their personal property will have relatively little value. An example might be when you buy a large screen television for several thousand dollars, several years later it may only be worth a few hundred dollars due to technological changes. With regard to personal property, it is always best for the couple to try to work out how they are going to share items rather than involving the Court or their attorneys. If the parties cannot come to an agreement there are methodologies used including alternating choices after flipping a coin to determine who goes first in selecting personal property.

Once the assets and liabilities are determined and valued, then they must be distributed. Either the parties can agree on the division of assets, or the court will award each asset and liability to one or the other party if an asset cannot be divided. The court will order that one person receive the asset and then order the receiving party to pay the non-receiving party a monetary award as determined by the court.

CUSTODY/VISITATION

Custody/visitation is the number one issue for most women who have children under the age of 18. The law of custody has gone from favoring mothers as care-taker of young children to being "gender" neutral. Either parent of a child starts with no presumption in his or her favor in a custody case. The court undertakes a custody decision by an analysis of a series of factors that, in their entirety, help the court determine the best interest of the child(ren). The factors that govern custody or visitation are outlined in Code of Va. § 20-124.3 reproduced here.

Virginia Child Custody - Best Interest of the Child - Va. Code § 20-124.3

Section 20-124.3 of the Virginia Code lists a number of factors that the judge should consider in deciding what is in the child's best interests. They are as follows:

1. *The age and physical and mental condition of the child and the child's developmental needs;*

2. *The age and physical and mental condition of each parent;*

3. *The relationship between each parent and the child, the parent's positive involvement and ability to assess and meet the child's needs;*

4. *The child's needs, including important relationships such as with brothers and sisters, grandparents, and other relatives;*

5. The role which each parent has played and will play in the upbringing and care of the child;

6. The propensity of each parent to actively support the child's contact and relationship with the other parent, including whether a parent has unreasonably denied the other parent access to or visitation with the child. **Note**-The courts seem to give extra weight to this factor.

7. Each parent's willingness to support the child's relationship with the other parent, their willingness and ability to maintain a close relationship with the child, and their ability to cooperate in matters affecting the child.

8. The child's preference (the weight of this will depend on the age and maturity of the child. There is no age at which a minor child can be the one who decides).

9. Any history of abuse; and

10. Any other factors the judge may feel necessary to consider.

There are actually several Code sections that one should read discussing custody, visitation, relocation, and even access to a child's records. §20-107.2, §20-124.1 thru §20-124.6.

There are basically two types of custody: Legal and Physical. Legal custody determines who has the right to make major decisions affecting how the child is going to be raised. Normally, the courts award joint legal custody, which essentially means that both parents will jointly make major decisions regarding the child. The major decisions contemplated involve education, religion and non-emergency medical care. Normally, education is not a contested issue because most children go to public school. If you want a child to go to a private school or a particularly expensive daycare program, and you intend for your spouse to pay some part of the bill, then he must be included in the decision-making process and agree to the child's placement. With matters of religion, the court is more limited due to Constitutional constraints. Normally, the child will continue the religious education and upbringing that was in place when the parents were living together.

The third subject of joint legal custody, medical care, really deals with decisions made regarding large medical expenditures or surgeries. Obviously, the child is going to the emergency room if an emergency arises, and will continue to have regular check-ups. Joint decisions would include decisions about medication, medical care or elective surgery. If one parent wants one outcome and the other one does not, then the courts may have to determine what care the child will receive.

Sole legal custody means that one parent has the right to make all decisions regarding the child, except for decisions that are otherwise ordered by the court. For instance, if you have sole custody, and the court has awarded visitation, then the sole custodian is bound by the order of the court and cannot decide to move outside the jurisdiction of the court, or make other major decisions that would alter the court order without seeking a change to the court's order. Sole custody is not normally awarded, unless the parties agree, or if there is child abuse, drug abuse, or some major problem which adversely affects the child such as two parents who cannot work together for the sake of the child.

Once the decision has been rendered as to sole legal custody or joint legal custody, the court then turns to physical custody. Physical custody determines with whom the child resides. The types of physical custody really have more to do with the amount of time the child spends with each parent. If the children have more than ninety overnight twenty four hour visits with each parent, then that is determined to be shared custody. One of the issues inherent with shared custody is the fact that child support is based, in part, on the custodial arrangement and particularly when the parenting arrangement provides that both parents have more than ninety days of visitation. The child support paid to the parent who has the most time with the child is often reduced due to shared custody support guidelines, since the other parent likewise has financial responsibilities to take care of the child. The effect of shared custody on child support is one of the toughest dilemmas facing a custodial parent when it adversely affects how one is to cover the expenses of raising a child.

Another form of custody is split custody, where one or more children live with one parent and another child or children live primarily with the other parent. While the courts do not favor split custody, there are times when the children are deemed better off being split between parents. Parenting time can be scheduled so that the children living in different households can spend time together with a certain frequency each month.

The most important advice I suggest to women with regard to custody is to recognize that each family is different and there is no "right" custodial arrangement. What works for one family may not work for the next. What is clear; however, is that children appear to do better when they have time with each parent and when the children have some input into the determination of custodial arrangements.

There are many issues involved in the custodial realm which need to be discussed in detail with an attorney. The issue of relocation is of concern to the courts because any such move interferes with the ability of the child to have a satisfactory relationship with the other parent. Grandparent rights, the rights of stepparents, and legal emancipation of a child before reaching eighteen are also very important issues that parents face which require clear guidance from both mental health professionals and attorneys.

When dealing with parenting issues, it is important for the parents to figure out how to communicate with one another in their rearranged family structure. Divorce need not be the destruction of a family relationship, but merely a rearrangement of how the family works.

With regard to relocation, the court requires that each parent give thirty days' advance written notice to the court and to the other parent if one intends to relocate or change his or her address. This is a very important provision.

Each parent has the right of access to the academic, medical, hospital, or other health records of that parent's minor child, unless it is otherwise ordered by the court for cause shown.

IMPORTANT - THE CARDINAL RULES ABOUT CUSTODY

1. "The best interest of the child" is the guiding principle in custody cases. Because the best interest of the child means something different to every participant in a custody trial, don't presume your point of view is the same as the judge's.

2. Always refer to the children as "our" children, not "my" children or "my" child.

3. Never, ever, ever, talk disparagingly about the child's father to or in the presence of one of your children. If your child asks you a question and the honest answer requires you to address a less than

flattering aspect of your spouse, speak to your child's therapist about how to best respond.

4. The court knows that you and your husband may differ in your philosophies of how to raise the children. The court realizes that you have differences in how rules are enforced, how you punish the children, and how you treat the children. The court does not intend to impose one parenting style over the other, so try and communicate and work with your soon-to-be ex. If you cannot communicate with your husband about the children, then talk with a children's mental health expert about how to handle specific issues.

5. If you believe that you are going to be in a contested custody case, you need to see an attorney experienced in contested custody cases immediately, so this person can give you advice on what to do, and just as importantly, what not to do.

6. Courts look disapprovingly at restricting access to a child. Possibly the biggest reason a father would win custody is if the mother had custody and restricted the child's access to his father.

7. Introducing new boyfriends and girlfriends into the life of a child before being divorced is potentially dangerous and damaging to your child and therefore to your custody case. Short answer: Don't do it!

8. Unless the father is abusive, have a picture of her or his father in the child's room.

9. Never deny visitation because you have not received the child support check. In the eyes of the court, the two are unrelated and it is deemed unreasonable to deny visitation even to a nonpaying father.

10. Custody is about CHILDREN, not fault. Use words like *Co-Parenting, parenting time*, not *custody* or *visitation*, when speaking with your husband.

11. Never ever, ever move out and temporarily leave your children with their dad. This is a sure way to lose physical custody.

12. Don't move out with the children unless you have a detailed plan of action coordinated with your attorney and even then, you are at risk of losing physical custody.

13. If you are in a romantic relationship, do not have your romantic partner spend the night when the children are there, even if you think they don't know because they are asleep.

14. Even if your husband's weekends with the children are your first nights off in years, resist the urge to jump start your social life and/or heal your broken heart by frequent late nights out. It will be used against you.

15. Do not let off steam by venting to your children's teachers, coaches, etc. about your ex. You do not want to appear the angry ex in court.

Good custody lawyers have access to various tech-nologies which can aid them and you meaningfully in preparing for your custody case. Ask your custody lawyer, or divorce lawyer, to demonstrate to you the various technologies they have available to help you win your case.

Aside from your attorney, the internet is the number one provider of information to fathers trying to obtain custody. One merely has to Google "father's rights" or "children's rights" to see the vast amount of informa-tion that is available online to parents. Your divorce at-torney should be able to provide *you* websites that will help you in your case.

CHILD SUPPORT

Virginia has adopted a child support model that is formulaic and is based on the number of children and the relative incomes of the parties. The statute govern-ing child support is 20-108.1, .2 and 20-107.2. If you are interested in determining how child support is cal-culated, please go to *www.dss.virginia.gov/family/dcse_calc.cgi*. For purposes of determining child support, we have included a child support guideline worksheet and filled in an example of how it works with the mother making $2000 per month and the father making $6,000 per month. In our example, the wife receives $520.00 spousal support, there are two children, and the monthly amount of healthcare coverage paid by father through his employer for just the children's portion is $150 per month. Child care is after school and costs approximately $120 per month. Based on those factors, as worked out on the child support guidelines, child support is $1006.00. The court can deviate from the guidelines in special circumstances, but this is highly unusual.

COMBINED SUPPORT WORKSHEET   v. _____

Fairfax Guideline Spousal and Child Support

Chancery No. _____

Worksheet of: _____   Date: _____

Child support is payable for: _2_ children.   Ages: _____

A. GROSS INCOME OF PARTIES		Mother/Wife	Father/Husband
1. Monthly Gross Income of Each Party:		$2,000	$6,000
2. Adjustment for Support of "Other Children":			
3. Adjustment for Self-Employment Tax:			
4. Adjusted Gross Incomes of Parties:		$2,000	$6,000
5. Combined Adjusted Income:	$8,000		

Payor Spouse
- ● Husband
- ○ Wife

B. SPOUSAL SUPPORT			
1. Payor Spouse's Adjusted Income:		$6,000	
2. Payor's Income X 28%			$1,680
3. Payee Spouse's Adjusted Income:		$2,000	
4. Payee's Income X 58%			$1,160
5. Guideline Spousal Support: (Line 2 Minus Line 4):			
6. Proposed Adjustments to Spousal Support:			

Uses The 28% - 58% Fairfax Guideline Formula.

Guideline Spousal Support
$520

7. Proposed Spousal Support Payable to:	Wife

Adjusted Spousal Support
$520

C. CHILD SUPPORT

Incomes with Guideline Adjustments including Spousal Support

Custodian
- ● Mother
- ○ Father

	Combined	Mother	Father
Adjusted Gross Incomes:	$8,000	$2,520	$5,480
		Income Shares	
Each Party's Percent of Combined Gross Income:	31.5%		68.5%
1. Schedule Amount for Basic Child Support:			$1,418
2. Work-related Child Care Costs:			$120
3. Medical Insurance for Child/Children:			$150
4. Total Child Support Need (Sum: 1+2+3+4):			

From Support Table

Child Support Need
$1,688

		Mother	Father
5. Child Support Obligation of Each Party:			
(Total support need X Income Share):		$532	$1,156
6. Direct Payment of Medical Insurance:			($150)
7. Each Party's Presumptive Guideline Share:		$532	$1,006
8. Guideline Child Support Payable to:	Mother		
9. Proposed Deviations From Guideline Support:			
10. Each Party's Proposed Share:		$532	$1,006
11. Proposed Adjusted Child Support Payable to:	Mother		

Guideline Child Support
$1,006

Adjusted Child Support
$1,006

D. Net Child and Spousal Support, Payable To:	Wife/Mother

NET SUPPORT
$1,526

Submitted by: _____

Counsel for: _____

11/12/05

RETIREMENTS

In Virginia, there is a formula to divide retirements, 401(k) plans, 403(b), 403 plans and other retirement related accounts.

The critical dates are the date of marriage and the date of separation. The formula for retirements is as follows: the numerator (number on top) is the total number years that husband/wife was employed with the company during the marriage to the date of separation. The denominator (or bottom number) is the total number of years employed with the company. That is multiplied by 50% times benefit received (or amount in the account).

FORMULA

Number of years employed
during the marriage to
date of separation X 50% X Amount in Retirement Account
Total number of years   Or Amount of Monthly benefit
husband employed by
Employer*

*If husband is still employed this number is unknown and we will use "Z" for "unknown"

EXAMPLE A: $100,000 in 401K
10 years of marriage to date
of separation
20 years of employment

<u>10</u> x 50% x amount in 401(K)
20

½ x ½ x 100,000=
.25 x 100,000 = $25,000

EXAMPLE B:
Monthly

3,000 Pension Payment

10 years marriage to date of
separation
20 years of employment

<u>10</u> x 50% x $3,000 =
20

5/10 x .50 x $3,000 =
½ x .50 x $3,000 =
.25 x $3,000 = $750.00 a month

There are issues such as what date one uses to value pensions and 401Ks that require more detailed discussion with your attorney.

Taxes. There are many tax implications regarding actions taken during a divorce which are not discussed in this book. You should have a tax discussion with your attorney and your accountant to ascertain possible tax issues that may arise in your divorce.

In Marriage And Divorce:
Look Before You Leap
15 Questions To Consider *Before* Hiring Your Divorce Lawyer

For most people, choosing a divorce lawyer is a daunting task. You are about to embark on an unfamiliar and treacherous journey through the legal system. And to make things worse, you have to do this while you are in the grip of extreme emotional turmoil.

Guiding you through this traumatic life experience should be a lawyer who you can trust completely, and with whom you can establish a close working relationship that will continue as long as you need, months, and in rare cases, even years.

Throughout the selection process, remind yourself that all lawyers are not created equal. Protect yourself by carefully considering the following fifteen questions before parting with that retainer check:

1. **Is the lawyer's practice focused exclusively on family law?**

Choose a lawyer who exclusively, or at least primarily, practices in the area of matrimonial and family law. This is a constantly evolving, highly complex area of practice. You need a knowledgeable and experienced lawyer in your corner who is intimately familiar with the intricacies of divorce law and related matters. You cannot leave the welfare of your children and your future financial security in the hands of a "Jack of All Trades, Master of None."

2. **Is the lawyer attentive when you are talking?**

It is crucial to have a face-to-face initial consultation with any potential lawyer before signing a retainer agreement. An initial consultation is a golden opportunity to assess whether the attorney will treat you with compassion and dedication, or whether you will be just another number in his book and a faceless file stacked in the corner of his cluttered office. If the lawyer is checking his e-mails, typing away on his Blackberry, or taking other calls during your meeting, you should go elsewhere.

3. **Does the lawyer have an office policy ensuring the timely return of you phone calls?**

Communication between attorney and client is key in any divorce action. A lawyer should be reachable by phone and e-mail. Unfortunately, clients' main complaints against their divorce lawyers are that the lawyers fail to respond in a timely manner to their calls, e-mails, and other communications. Ask any lawyer you consider retaining whether there is an office policy regarding the prompt return of phone calls and emails. If the lawyer hesitates, there most likely is no such policy, and you will be frustrated to no end in trying to get in touch with him or her.

4. Is the lawyer selective in accepting cases?

Does the lawyer you are considering accept every client that walks through the door, or does his or her practice consist of fewer, but select, clients? In order to provide dedicated and comprehensive service, an attorney owes it to existing clients to be highly selective in accepting new matters. Make sure that is the case with your attorney.

5. Is your personality compatible with the lawyer's personality?

In order to work effectively with your lawyer, you must be comfortable with him or her. Make sure that the lawyer you retain is someone with whom you can talk, to whom you can listen, and with whom you will be able to share the most intimate details of your life and finances without feeling threatened in any way.

6. Does the lawyer treat you with compassion and empathy?

Make sure that the lawyer treats you as the unique individual that you are. A good lawyer will be eager to listen to your marital history and will make sure to fully understand your priorities and objectives without being in a rush to help you into categories or hurry you out the door.

7.   Is the lawyer proactive?

You should hire a divorce lawyer who is able to provide you with a plan of action. This attorney should listen to you and then take charge.

8.   Will the lawyer handle you case personally, or will your matter be delegated to an associate or paralegal?

Find out who will handle your case. Will it be the attorney you are meeting with during the initial consultation? If any portion of your case is going to be delegated to an associate or paralegal, you should insist on meeting that lawyer or paralegal as well. You must be completely satisfied that any other staff member working on your case is competent and experienced. This is essential.

9.   Is the lawyer willing to attempt a negotiated settlement of your matter?

Only a very small percentage of divorce cases actually go to trial. The vast majority of cases are settled, some on the court house steps on the very day of trial. A good attorney knows that there is no "winner" in a divorce or custody trial. If it is left unchecked, the process can be emotionally and financially devastating to both parties. Your attorney should, therefore, make every reasonable effort to negotiate a settlement on your behalf, while at the same time diligently preparing your case for the potentiality of a trial. Cases settle when the lawyers are prepared and dedicated.

10. Is the lawyer willing to educate you and to answer your questions?

Your divorce lawyer must be a good communicator and be willing to answer all of your questions. Any skilled divorce lawyer knows that educated clients are better equipped to make sound and informed decisions with regard to their and their families' futures.

11. Is the lawyer assertive without being arrogant?

Many people make the mistake of looking for a divorce lawyer that will be a "pit-bull." In hiring a divorce lawyer, remember that louder does not necessarily mean better. A good attorney will not feel the need to compensate for a lack of skill by being obnoxious. A good attorney will aggressively and effectively advocate for you, but without an ego that squeezes the air out of any room.

12. Is the lawyer being honest with you, or are you being promised the sun, the moon, and the stars?

Be very wary of any lawyer who guarantees a specific result in your divorce case. All litigation is inherently risky and can be influenced by present circumstances, future developments, and the decisions and attitude of the judge. Every case has strengths and weaknesses, and your lawyer should point out both. You can trust an attorney who tells it like it is–who is candid with you about your chances of obtaining a particular outcome. You cannot trust an attorney who simply tells you what you want to hear.

13. Does the lawyer underscore that your children's best interest are your highest priorities?

No parent should ever use children as pawns in a divorce action. Your children's welfare and best interest should be your paramount priority. Any good lawyer will understand and support this objective and will caution you that manipulating your children will be devastating to them personally and to your chances of being awarded custody.

14. Does the lawyer present himself or herself well?

If you are put off by your lawyer's personal grooming, dress, behavior, or language, chances are that the judge and opposing counsel will be too. If a lawyer's office is a mess of paper, pizza boxes, and dirty clothes, the legal documents that he or she prepares on your behalf will most likely reflect that. The work product on your case will not be thoughtful, cogent and organized either. You want an attorney who cares enough to present himself or herself, the staff, and the office in a professional manner.

15. Is the lawyer able to utilize the latest technology?

In this day and age, your lawyer should be up-to-date on the latest technological developments. Your lawyer should understand how computers, the internet, PDAs, etc. are changing communications, relationships and society. He or she should be aware of the implications of this. If a lawyer has chosen to remain blindly "old school" about technology, do you think he or she cares enough to stay up-to-date with the latest developments in the law?

If you need to hire a divorce lawyer, be sure to do your homework and to consider these questions before signing a retainer agreement. The last thing you need during your divorce case is to waste your precious energy on disagreements with your lawyer. So, be sure to hire the right lawyer right from the start and save yourself the agony of lost time, big bills, and endless frustration.

"TAKE AS MUCH TIME TO PLAN YOUR DIVORCE AS YOU DID TO PLAN YOUR WEDDING."

STEPS TO PREPARE FOR DIVORCE

1. Attend the **"What Women Need to Know About Divorce"** seminars on the 2nd Saturday of every month at 8:30 am and the 3rd Tuesday of every month at 6:30 p.m. The seminars are held at two locations on Saturdays : the Friends Meeting House, 1537 Laskin Road (across from Hilltop East Shopping Center) in Virginia Beach; and at the Extended Stay America Hotel, 809 Greenbrier Circle, near the Chesapeake Conference Center. The seminar is held in Virginia Beach only on Tuesday evenings, at the Friends Meeting House. Consult an attorney about your legal rights.

2. Write a narrative for your attorney, detailing the date you began living together, the date you married, your children's birth dates, previous separations, when various assets were acquired, and the separate property either of you brought into the marriage or inherited.

3. Gather information about what you own and owe. You'll need copies of financial statements, tax returns, retirement plan documents, brokerage statements and insurance policies.

4. Obtain detailed information on each retirement plan in which you and your husband have participated.

5. Decide which assets you would like to keep if you divorce and what you are willing to give up. Consult with your accountant about the tax consequences of various options, especially of keeping the house.

6. Get preliminary estimates of the value of the property you own and list the debts that you owe. Pay bills and credit cards from joint funds before separation, so you don't get stuck with them later.

7. Find out what is in the safe deposit box. Secure both keys, if possible.

8. Prepare a spending history for last year from your checkbooks so you can determine future needs and decide where to cut back if necessary.

9. Before you separate, use joint funds to repair your automobile and home, buy clothes for yourself and your children, and get needed dental work and medical checkups. If you wait until after separation, those expenses will be yours alone.

10. Set aside cash reserves to use in the first few months of separation. Transfer your share of joint funds to your separate bank account.

11. Apply for credit cards in your own name. If possible, obtain credit cards with check writing privileges.

12. After separation, close joint credit card accounts, get control of both cards issued on accounts, or notify creditors that you will ho longer be responsible for your husband's charges on accounts.

13. Open a post office box that you can use for your mail before you separate and while you are in the process of divorce.

14. Begin a divorce notebook in which you list all problems with impending separation and divorce. Also list each step that you take in the divorce process, including a synopsis of all telephone calls and conferences with your attorney and accountant. Keep good notes.

15. Divorce is scary, but it will be less so if you figure out the worst that could happen and decide in advance how you will deal with it. Investigate community resources that are available to you.

16. Explore your career options. Use the crisis of divorce to catapult yourself into a more satisfying future.

17. Begin negotiation discussions with your husband, as calmly as possible. Find out what his hot buttons are and where he is willing to make concessions.

18. Attend family law court proceedings and talk to family and friends who have been through divorce recently. Get a feel for the territory you will be crossing.

19. Find a good therapist or support group to help you through the months ahead. Divorce is too traumatic to go through it alone.

20. Take your time and don't rush matters. Planning for divorce is best done deliberately and slowly. This is your chance for a new beginning.

Special Thanks to Giuita Wall, CFP of San Diego, California for allowing me to develop the "Second Saturday" seminar on the east coast and for allowing me to use this "steps to prepare for divorce" since 1990.

FINANCIAL RECORDS WITH WHICH EVERY WOMAN SHOULD BE FAMILIAR

1. Net Worth Statement
2. Copies of all notes signed by yourself and your husband (Include 1st and 2nd mortgages)
3. Copies of any guarantees on behalf of others signed by you or your spouse
4. Tax returns for the last 3 years
5. Benefit statements of your employer and spouse's employer (pension plan, profit sharing, 401K, IRA, etc.)
6. Life insurance policies on you, your spouse and children
7. Short term disability policies on you and your spouse
8. Long term disability policies on you and your spouse
9. Homeowner's policy
10. Umbrella liability policy
11. Car insurance policies
12. Health insurance policies
13. Long term care insurance policies
14. Other insurance policies (Mortgage payment, credit life, AAA policy, cancer policy, etc.)

15. All bank account statements
16. All credit card statements
17. All brokerage statements
18. Any military benefits
19. Copy of credit history (obtain from retail merchants and any other applicable agencies)
20. Inventory of personal property (written and video)
21. Applicable employment contracts
22. Copies of buy sell agreements
23. Copies of Partnership Agreements
24. Inventory of lock box
25. Power of Attorney for you and your spouse
26. Medical Power of Attorney for Babysitters
27. Durable Medical Power of Attorney for you and your spouse
28. Wills
29. Living Wills
30. Copies of any Wills or Trusts of which you are the beneficiary
31. Trusts
32. Social Security Benefits Statement
33. Pre Nuptial Agreements
34. Separation Agreements
35. Lease Agreements
36. Real Estate Contracts
37. Mutual Fund statements
38. Annuity Statements

THE HIGH COST OF
DIVORCE VS. THE IRS

- Legal fees and court costs for getting a divorce are generally personal and non-deductible; however, professional fees paid for tax advice or to obtain a taxable spousal support award will be deductible on your tax return in the year paid, under the provisions of Internal Revenue Code Sec. 212, since they are attributable to determination of taxes or the production of income.

- Legal fees spent to increase spousal support payments or collect arrearages are also deductible, under the same theory, but that deductibility doesn't extend to the paying spouse. His legal costs incurred while attempting to reduce support payments or to defend against a claim for greater support are not deductible by him.

- Legal fees are only deductible by the person who incurs them. Legal fees are never deductible where one spouse is ordered to pay the other spouse's legal fees, since a taxpayer is allowed a deduction only for the costs of advice to him or her, not for advice to the other party.

- Even the portion of your legal expenses that is not currently tax-deductible may become deductible when you sell assets you receive. A portion of your attorney fees can be allocated among the different assets that you receive in the settlement and will be added to the tax basis of each. You must be able to show that those fees were for time spent defending title to assets or obtaining them for you. For example, the cost of preparing and filing a deed to put title to a property in your name alone can be added to the tax basis of the property and deducted when the property is sold.

- In order to claim a deduction for legal expenses incurred in a divorce, the attorney must make a reasonable allocation of the legal expenses between deductible and non-deductible advice. The allocation may be in the form of an opinion letter from the attorney, based on reliable time records of services rendered. Any fees paid to a specialized professional, such as a tax attorney or CPA, for tax and investment advice will be fully deductible. The best evidence of deductible fees is a statement appearing directly on the attorney's bills regarding the portion attributable to tax advice, securing taxable support, and obtaining assets.

- The fees that are currently deductible, such as those for tax advice or those for securing income, can only be claimed if you itemize deductions on Schedule A of Form 1040. They are claimed as miscellaneous deductions and are subject to the 2% of adjusted gross income floor.

- The costs of personal advice, custody issues, counseling, or legal action in a divorce are not deductible. It may be difficult to separate the non-deductible personal costs of divorce from the deductible costs, but if the potential deduction is sizeable, the additional effort required to ferret out the tax-deductible portion will be worthwhile.

2ND SATURDAY - WHAT WOMEN NEED TO KNOW ABOUT DIVORCE RESOURCE LIST

ABUSE
BATTERED WOMEN'S HOTLINES, SHELTERS, SUPPORT GROUPS, AND INFORMATION

National Resource Center for Domestic Violence	800-537-2238
National Domestic Violence Hotline (24 hour)	800-799-7233
Family Violence & Sexual Assault Hotline of VA	800-838-8238
Response Crises Hotline	757-622-4300
Center for Sexual Assault Survivors	757-599-9848
Norfolk: YWCA (Women in Crisis Program, shelter, etc.) Support Group-	
Call for dates & times	757-625-5570
Union Mission Family Shelter	757-623-0642
Virginia Beach: Samaritan House & Safe Harbor Center Support Group	
	757-631-0710
Judeo Christian Outreach Center	757-491-2846
Chesapeake/Portsmouth: Hershelter (Help and Emergency Response Support Group	
- Call for dates & times	757-485-3384
Suffolk: Genieve Shelter	800-969-4673
Hampton: Transitions Family Violence Services Support Group - Call for dates & times	
	757-723-7774
Williamsburg: Avalon	757-258-5051
Gloucester: Laurel Shelter	804-694-5552

Victim/Witness Assistance Programs

Accomack County	757-787-8538
Chesapeake	757-382-6417
Gloucester County	757-693-1227
Hampton	757-727-6442
Isle of Wight County	757-357-7403
Newport News	757-926-7443
Norfolk	757-664-4850
Portsmouth	757-393-8729
Suffolk	757-923-2222
Virginia Beach	757-385-8301
York County / Poquoson	757-890-3402
Yorktown	757-890-3401
Matthews	804-725-1291

Battered Women Support Groups

Chesapeake/Portsmouth — Battered Women's Support Group - Hershelter
757-485-3384 or 757-382-8172

Norfolk — Battered Women's Support Group - YWCA Women
in Crisis Program — 757-625-4248

Hampton — Transitions Family Violence Services
757-723-7774

Isle of Wight County — Victim Witness Program Support Group
757-357-7403

Virginia Beach Domestic Violence Police Unit (M - F 8am - 12 midnight)
757- 385-4101

Pace (Police Assisted Community Enforcement) Norfolk Social Services Department
757-664-6016

Child Abuse Information

Prevent Child Abuse Hampton Roads   757-440-2749

Virginia Child Abuse and Neglect Hotline-VA Dept. of Social Services 800-552-7096

Prevent Child AbuseVirginia   800-244-5373

National Child Abuse Hotline - Child Help USA   800-422-4453

Norfolk Child Abuse and Neglect (24 hour)-Child Protective Services 757-664-6022

FACTS (Families of Abused Children Traumatized Sexually)-Vera Dammert 757-481-9521

DOMESTIC VIOLENCE ADVOCACY UNITS, COURT INTAKE AND CLERKS, MAGISTRATES

Accomack County J & D Court Clerk	757-787-0920
Chesapeake	
J & D Court	
Intake	757-382-8150 or
	757-382-8170
Clerk	757-382-8100
Magistrate	757-382-6632
Franklin City J & D Court Clerk	757-562-8559
James City County /Williamsburg	
J & D Court Clerk	757-564-2200
Hampton	
J & D Court	
Intake	757-727-6357
Clerk	757-727-6147
Magistrate	757-727-6589
Isle of Wight County	
J & D Court Clerk	757-365-6237

Newport News
  J & D Court
      Intake   757-926-8781
      Clerk   757-926-3603
  Magistrate   757-926-8475
Norfolk
  SAFE (Spousal Abuse Friend & Educator Program)   757-664-7647
  Friends of the Norfolk Juvenile Court, Inc.   757-664-7649
  J & D Court
      Intake   757-664-7610
      Clerk   757-664-7340
  Magistrate   757-664-4799
Northampton County
  J & D Court Clerk   757-678-0466
Portsmouth
  FAIR (Friendly Advocates in Intimate Relationships)   757-397-2799
  Friends of the Portsmouth Juvenile Court   757-397-2799
  J & D Court
      Intake   757-393-8571
      Clerk.   757-393-8851
  Magistrate   757-393-8648
Southampton County J & D Court Clerk.   757-653-2673
Suffolk
  J & D Court   757-514-7790
  Court Services Unit   757-514-4311
  Magistrate   757-514-4301
Virginia Beach
  FANS (Family Advocacy Network Services)   757-426-5607
  J & D Court
      Intake   757-385-4361 or
            757-385-4362
      Clerk   757-385-4391
  Magistrate   757-385-4724

MILITARY RESOURCES

American Legion Family Support Network Hotline (financial and family assistance)

	800-504-4098
Ex-Pose (Ex-Partners of Servicemen [Women] for Equality)	757-499-5386

Fleet and Family Support Centers - www.ffscnorva.navy.mil

Naval Amphibious Base, Little Creek	757-462-7563
Naval Base, Norfolk	757-444-2102
Chesapeake, NW	757-421-8770
Naval Air Station, Oceana	757-433-2912
Naval Weapons Station, Yorktown	757-887-4606
Newport News Shipbuilding	757-688-6289

New Parent Support Program Offices

Langley AFB	757-222-7130 ext. 3
Langley AFB Family Advocacy Program	757-764-2427

Navy Family Advocacy (addresses prevention, identification, treatment, follow-up & reporting child abuse, neglect & spouse abuse)

Naval Amphibious Base, Little Creek	757-462-7563
Family Advocacy Social Worker (After Hours)	757-953-5008
Naval Air Station, Oceana	757-.433-2555 or 757-433-2558
Naval Base, Norfolk	757-444-2230
Naval Medical Center, Portsmouth	757-953-7801
Naval Weapons Station, Yorktown	757-887-4301
Naval Security Group Activity, NW - Chesapeake	757-421-8770

Navy Legal Assistance Offices

Naval Amphibious Base, Little Creek	757-462-4759
Naval Station, Norfolk	757-444-5300 or 757-444-5053
Naval Air Station, Oceana	757-433-2230 ext. 223
Naval Medical Center, Portsmouth	757-953-5452
Naval Legal Assistance Dept.	757-444-5300 or 757-444-5303

www.militaryK12link.com (Hampton Roads school info - includes localities, transferal info, etc. - part of Fleet and Family Support)

Tri - Care (Military Medical HMO)	757-953-6708

Army: Soldiers & Family Support Center

Ft. Eustis	757-878-0901
Ft. Monroe	757-788-3878
Ft. Story	757-422-7311

Langley AFB Airmen & Family Readiness Center	757-764-3990
Langley AFB Family Advocacy	757-764-9581
Langley AFB Legal Assistance	757-788-3616

USCG EAP Program - Yorktown	757-856-2161
US Coast Guard Integrated Support Command - Family Advocacy	757-686-4020
USCG MLCLANT (Legal Assistance)	757-628-4213

Navy - Marine Corps Relief Society (primarily for financial counseling)

Norfolk Office	757-423-8830
Little Creek Office	757-464-9364
Oceana Office	757-433-3383
Portsmouth Office	757-953-5956

COMMUNITY RESOURCES

Second Saturday - What Women Need to Know About Divorce - Voice Mail Hotline	757-456-1574
United Way (Family, financial counseling & other extensive services)	
Norfolk Understanding People Center	757-622-7017
Portsmouth	757-397-2121
Information and Referral Services of the Planning Council	757-625-4543
ODU Women's Center	757-683-4109

TCC Regional Women's Center
    Portsmouth Campus   757-822-2160
    Norfolk Campus   757-822-1140
    Chesapeake Campus   757-822-5133
    Virginia Beach Campus   757-822-7363
Virginia Wesleyan College   757-455-3200
Departments of Social Services
    Chesapeake   757-382-2000
    Hampton   757-727-1800
    James City County   757-259-3100
    Newport News (Denbeigh office)   757-396-3160
    Newport News (Jefferson Avenue office)   757-926-6300
    Norfolk   757-664-6000
    Portsmouth   757-405-1800
    Suffolk   757-923-3000
    Virginia Beach   757-437-3200
    Williamsburg   757-220-6161
    York County/Poquoson   757-890-8737
Virginia Department of Social Services (Eastern Region - VA Beach field office)
    757-491-3990
Division of Child Support Enforcement Pendleton Child Service Center
    757-437-2100
Community Services Board - City of Virginia Beach
    Mental Health Emergency Services   757-385-0888
    Child and Youth Services
        MESA Mutual Education Support & Advocacy
    757-385-0802
        MST In-Home Services   757-385-0834
        Outpatient Child and Youth   757-437-6200
Community Services Board - City of Norfolk   757-441-5300
Community Services Board - City of Chesapeake   757-547-9334
Catholic Charities of Eastern VA   757-467-7707
Jewish Family Services of Tidewater   757-459-4640
United Methodist Family Services of Virginia   757-490-9791

DIVORCE/SEPARATION GROUPS

Divorce Care at King's Grant Baptist Church, Va Beach, co -ed
(call for dates and times)   757-340-0902
Divorce Care at Avalon Church of Christ, Va Beach, co-ed
(call for dates and times)   757-420-5208
Divorce Care at London Bridge Baptist Church, co-ed
(call for dates and times)   757-486-7900
Divorce Care at Ascension Catholic Church   757-499-0843
Divorce Recovery Group at First Baptist Church of Norfolk, co -ed,
call for information   757-461-3226
Starting Over (Ministry for separated, divorced or widowed individuals)
                                                             757-499-0843

PARENTING, COUPLES,
CHILDREN'S RESOURCES

Barry Robinson Center - A Behavioral Health System for Youth
                                        757-455-6100 or 800-221-1995
Child Help USA   800-4ACHILD
Children in the Middle (support group for children of divorcing parents - Jewish Family Services of Tidewater)   757-459-4640
Compassionate Friends (Bereavement support group for parents who have lost a child/children)   757-482-5856
YMCA Parenting Programs (Variety of parent support groups plus classes for parents of younger children and teens)   757-622-9622
Parents Without Partners   757-545-0386 or 757-498-2666
PAIRS (Intensive, comprehensive, dynamic classes for couples' skill building & relationship work) - contact Marc Rabinowitz   757-622-9852
PREP (Marriage Enrichment Program offered by YMCA Parenting Programs
                                                             757-622-9622
Seton House (Runaway Teen Support, Shelter and Counseling) 24 hour hotline
                                        757-498-HELP or 757-498-4357
Happily Parenting Teens (Seton House)   757-306-1840

Grandparents as Parents Support Group - GAP (Catholic Charities of Hampton Roads)
757-456-2366
Kids Cope - Catholic Family Services - for children 6 - 12;
dealing with divorce and separation   757-467-7707
Kids Priority One - excellent resource for all things concerning family
in the community   757-244-5373
www.militaryK12link.com (Hampton Roads school info, includes localities, trans-
ferral info, etc. - part of Navy Fleet and Family Support

CHILD SUPPORT ENFORCEMENT

STATE   www.dss.state.va.us/family/dcseoffices.cgi   800-481-1004

LEGAL RESOURCES

Approved Court mandated custody/parenting programs

And How Are the Children? (Presented by Pendleton Child Service Center)
757-385-4537
Children and Divorce (Presented by Navy Fleet and Family Support). call any FFSC
Children First - Chesapeake Volunteers in Youth Services   757-382-8184, intake
Cooperative Co-parenting Seminars (presented by Mediation Center
of Hampton Roads)   757-624-6666
Cooperative Co-parenting - issues surrounding separation and divorce
Catholic Charities of Eastern VA   757-467-7707

The UP Center Understanding People Program   757-622-7017

Legal Aid Society of Eastern Virginia
Hampton   757-275-0080
Norfolk   757-627-5423
Legal Services of Eastern Virginia (LSEVA)
Hampton   757-827-5078

Virginia Beach	757-552-0026
Williamsburg	757-220-6837
Eastern Shore (Bell Haven, VA)	757-442-3014
Lawyers Referral Service (Hampton Roads)	757-623-0132
Virginia Lawyer Referral Service	800-552-7977
Community Mediation Center -Mediation	757-480-2777
Mediation Center of Hampton Roads - Mediation	757-624-6666
Samaritan House	757-631-0710
Virginia Poverty Law Center	800-868-8752
Martindale-Hubbell Lawyer Locator at Public Law Library or online at	
	www.lawyers.com
Hofheimer/Ferrebee P.C., Representing Only Women in Custody and Divorce	757-425-5200
General legal information site - find attorneys, legal information, etc.	*www.lawinfo.com*
Virginia Bar Association	804-644-0041
Virginia State Bar Association	804-775-0500
Virginia Beach Bar Association	*www.vbbarassoc.com*
Information on all Virginia courts, by type and by city	*www.courts.state.va.us*
Metropolitan Richmond Women's Bar Association	*www.mrwba.org*

STAGES OF DIVORCE

It has been observed that divorcing persons move through a natural progression of stages of divorce. Every person experiences these stages differently. (Some may skip a stage or two). Since divorce adjustment has its roots in the marriage, that is where we will begin.

STAGE 1: DISILLUSIONMENT

Disillusionment begins when two spouses realize there are some very real differences between them. The person who is to fulfill almost all one's expectations, needs and ideals turns out to be depressed, sloppy, boring, unaffectionate, a social, uncaring, insensitive, etc., etc. While these thoughts and statements intrude on the happiest of marriages, prolonged time spent dwelling on them sows the seeds of destruction.

STAGE 2: EROSION

The state is characterized by a chipping away of each other's egos. One or the other says "I'm not getting enough out of this marriage." Sometimes, a careful vigilance is maintained to make sure that one does not give any more than the other. The concentration in this period is on taking rather than giving, being loved instead of loving. Sex becomes a battleground where frigidity or impotency expresses the frozen anger.

STAGE 3: DETACHMENT

In the detachment stage the couple no longer cares enough to hate or fight. Each feels a low commitment to the relationship; they barely talk, avoid physical affection or sex, don't look into the others' eyes, etc.

This period is not so much one of an intensified conflict as it is increasing boredom with the conflict. The coldness that was at first withholding of love has become habitual and natural. Empty hulls of people pass each other in routine. The detached person begins to dream of his or her own future without the spouse.

STAGE 4: PHYSICAL SEPARATION

For those who have spent a long time preparing to get divorced by building up the courage to leave an intolerable marriage, the physical separation can bring enormous relief. For those who are unprepared and still emotionally involved in the spouse, physical separation can leave a person in shock. But most all newly separated persons have to face the loneliness, anxiety, initial confusion and fears.

The American culture nourishes insidious fears of loneliness. Being alone with one's self represents nothingness, a void to most people. We are learning that loneliness can also be creative. Out of loneliness comes strong determination, courage and deep commitment. Anxiety is another common emotion following physical separation–fear of the unknown. The future is uncertain. Many divorcing individuals change their vacations, lifestyles, residences and friends. The separated person may worry about meeting financial needs, about being attractive to the opposite sex. about the effect of divorce on children, etc., etc.

Separation brings new anxieties.

STAGE 5: MOURNING

Mourning is a web of anger, hurt, loneliness, relief and helplessness. Mourning helps rid one's self of the ghosts. Person says "I can't go back . . . but I can't go forward." They want intimacy but feel they can't handle it. In this stage, the divorcing person moves from no goals to concrete goals. They will take off the wedding ring, rearrange the furniture and "clean out the old house," and begin as a single person.

Mourning during divorce may unleash anger. Releasing anger is a necessary part of divorce. Depression may also accompany mourning.

STAGE 6: SECOND ADOLESCENCE

Instead of looking back on the former spouse with anger and attraction the person during this stage is concentrating on his/her personal growth. Choices begin to increase. Vision clears. The excitement of possible new adventures and new risks creates an almost adolescent state. Previous areas of deprivation, whether sexual, travel, fun, hobbies, friends, or training are often vigorously pursued.

Dating often renews old adolescent feelings. "Is he/she going to call? Will he/she accept the invitation? Are my social skills ok according to today's standard?" A divorcing person may feel considerable intrigue and excitement during this stage.

STAGE 7: EXPLORATION AND HARD WORK

With renewed vitality, the divorcing individual begins earnestly to pursue self-chosen goals. Instead of seeing overwhelming, unreachable future aspirations, a plan of action toward manageable, reachable goals has been implemented. New relationships are formed, old ones with children are enhanced.

You may feel a new confidence, a sense of being master over your life.

Children's Age Appropriate Books On Divorce*

BOOKS FOR YOUR PRESCHOOLER

Dinosaurs Divorce: A Guide for Changing Families.
Brown, Laurene Krasny, and Brown, Marc,
Boston: Little, Brown, and Co., 1986.
Divorce. Rogers, Fred; Judkis, Jim. PaperStar Book,
1996.
Divorce. Tubs, Janet. Arcadia Press. 2000. (Ages 3-9)
Mama and Daddy Bear's Divorce. Spelman,
Cornelia Maude. Albert Whitman. 2001.
Mom and Dad Don't Live Together Anymore.
Stinson, Kathy. Annick Press. 1985.
*My Stick Family: Helping Children Cope with
Divorce.* Reilly, Natalie Jane. New Horizon
Press. 2003. (To be read to younger children)
Please Come Home. Sanford, Doris. Multomah Press. 1985.
Sometimes a Family Has to Split Up. Watson, Jane
Werner. Crown Publishers, Inc. 1988.
Two Houses. Masurel, Claire. Candlewick Press. 2003.

BOOKS FOR YOUR 5 TO 8 YEAR OLD

All Families Are Special. Simon, Norma. Albert
Whitman & Co. 2003.
All Kinds of Families. Simon, Norma. Albert
Whitman & Co. 1987.

At Daddy's on Saturdays. Girard, Linda. Albert Whitman & Co. 1991.

Break-Up. Padoan, Gianni. Milan, Italy: Child's Play, 1987.*Charlie Anderson.* Abercrombie, Barbara; Graham, Mark. Aladdin Publishing Company, 1995.

Daddy Doesn't Live Here Any More. Holmes, Margaret. Dorrance Publishing Co., 1996.

Daddy's New Baby. Vigna, Judith. Albert Whitman & Co. 1982.

Dinosaurs Divorce: A Guide for Changing Families. Brown, Laurene Krasny, and Brown, arc. Boston: Little, Brown, and Co., 1986.

Do I Have A Daddy? - A Story About A Single Parent. Lindsey, Jeanne W. Morning Glory Press. 2000.

Eliza's Daddy. Thomas, Ianthe. Harcourt. 1976.

Grandma without Me. Vigna, Judith. Albert Whitman & Co. 1984.

I Don't Want to Talk About It: A Story About Divorce for Young Children. Ransom, Jeanie Franz; Finney, Katherine Kuntz. American Psychological Association. 2000.

I Have Two Families. Helmering, Doris. Abington. 1981.

I Live with Daddy. Vigna, Judith. Albert Whitman & Co. 1997.

I Wish I Had My Father. Simon, Norma. Whitman. 1983.

*It's Not Your Fault, KoKo Bear: A Read-Together
Book for Parents and Young Children During
Divorce.* Book Peddlers. 1998.

Let's Talk About It B Stepfamilies. Rogers, Fred;
Judkis, Jim. Putnam Publishing Group. 2001.

Let's Talk About Your Parent's Divorce. Weitzman,
Elizabeth. Rosen Publishing Group. 2003 (Ages 8-9)

Like Jake and Me. Jukes, Mavis. Dragonfly Books.
1987.

Mom Is Dating Weird Wayne. Auch, Mary Jane.
Holiday House. 1988.

Mommy and Me by Ourselves. Vigna, Judith. Albert
Whitman & Co. 1987.

*My Family's Changing: A First Look at Family
Breakup.* Thomas, Pat. Barron's Educational
Series. 1999.

My Mom and Dad Are Getting a Divorce. Bienfield,
Florence. 1st Books Library. 2002.

On the Day His Daddy left. Adams, Eric J. Albert
Whitman & Co. 2003.

*Sailing through the Storm: A Child's Journey
through Divorce.* Julie, Edie. Kidsail. 1996.

She's Not My Real Mother. Vigna, Judith. Albert
Whitman & Co. 1987.

*Two Homes to Live In: A Child's-Eye View of
Divorce.* Hazen, Barbara Shook. Human
Sciences Press, Inc. 1983.

When Mom and Dad Divorce. Mememdez B Aponte.
Abbey Press. 1999.

Why Do Families Break Up? Bingham, Jane. Raintree Publishers. 2004.

BOOKS FOR YOUR PRETEEN

Amber Brown Sees Red. Danzinger, Paula. Scholastic. 1998.

Dear Mr. Henshaw. Cleary, Beverly. Morrow, 1983.

Divorce Express. Danziger, Paula. Delacorte, 1982.

Divorce Helpbook for Kids. MacGregor, Cynthia. Impact Publishers, Inc. 2001.

Divorce is not the End of the World. Stern, Zoe; Stern, Evan; Stern, Ellen Sue. Tricycle Press, 1997.

Don't Fall Apart on Saturdays! The Children's Divorce Survival Book. Moser, Adolph. Landmark Editions, 2000.

Don't Make Me Smile. Park, Barbara. Random House Children's Books. 2002.

Double Dare. Dower, Laura. Hyperion Books for Children. 2003. (from the Files of Madison Finn Series)

Hatchet. Paulsen, Gary. Scholastic. 1999.

Help! : A Girl's Guide to Divorce and Stepfamilies. Holyoke, Nancy. Pleasant Co. Communications. 1999.

How it feels when Parents Div orce. Krementz, Jill. Alfred A. Knopf. 1988.

It's Not the End of the World. Blume, Judy. New York: Dell, 1972. Reissue.

The Kids' Book of Divorce: By, For and About Kids.
Rofes, Eric. Lewis Publishing Co. 1981.
Mitzi's Honeymoon with Nana Potts. Williams,
Barbara. E. P. Dutton. 1983.
Mom Is Dating Weird Wayne. Auch, Mary Jane.
Holiday House. 1988.
*My Parents are Divorced Too: A Book for Kids by
Kids.* Ford, Melanie, et al. American
Psychological Assoc. 1998.
My Parents Are Getting Divorced Too. Cadier,
Florence. Abrahms, Harry N., Inc. 2004.
A Solitary Blue. Voight, Cynthia. Aladdin Publishing
Co. 2003. Reissue.
Strider. Cleary Beverly. Harper Trophy. 1992.
*What in the World Do You Do When Your Parents
Divorce?* : A Survival Guide for Kids. Beyer,
Roberta; Winchester, Kent. Free Spirit
Publications, Inc. 2001.
What's Going to Happen to Me? Le Shan, Eda. Four
Winds, 1978.

BOOKS FOR YOUR TEEN

*Broken Hearts*YHealing: Young Poets Speak Out on
Divorce. Worthen, Tom, ed. Poet Tree Press UT.
2001.
Divorce Express. Danziger, Paula. Putnam Juvenile.
1997. Reprint.
Divorce Handbook for Teens. MacGregor, Cynthia.
Impact Publishers, Inc. 2004.

Charles R. Hofheimer, Esq.

Divorce is not the End of the World. Stern, Zoe; Stern, Evan; Stern, Ellen Sue. Tricycle Press. 1997.

Don't Fall Apart on Saturdays! The Children's Divorce Survival Book. Moser, Adolph. Landmark Editions. 2000.

Father Figure. Peck, Richard. Puffin Books. 1996.

How it Feels When Parents Divorce. Krementz, Jill. Alfred A. Knopf. 1988.

Moonlight Man, The. Fox, Paula. New York: Dell, 1988.

Stepkids: A Survival Guide for Teenagers in Stepfamilies. Getzoff, Ann; McClenahan, Carolyn. Walker and Co. 1984.

A Tangle of Roots. Girion, Barbara. Putnam. 1985.

* Special Thanks to Dr. Lynn Zoll who provided this list of books to us in 2004. Dr. Lynn Zoll's email address is mollypaws20@gmail.com.

ABOUT THE AUTHOR

Virginia Divorce Attorney Charles R. Hofheimer has devoted much of his career protecting the interests of thousands of women contemplating or confronting divorce or contested custody cases.

Since 1990 Charlie has conducted monthly three-hour seminars on "What Women Need to Know About Divorce." His seminar program, locally known as "Second Saturday," has been recognized by the Virginia State Bar for its outreach to the women of Virginia, especially in the cities of Virginia Beach and Chesapeake, Virginia.

Charlie has held numerous professional positions including Chairman of the Family Law Section of the Virginia Trial Lawyers Association for two successive terms, founding member of the Virginia College of Trial Advocacy, founding member and past chair of the Virginia Institute of Collaborative Professionals, founding member and past chair of Virginia Collaborative Professionals, a statewide organization promoting multidisciplinary team collaborative divorce, and emeritus member of the Hoffman I'Anson Inn of Court.

Mr. Hofheimer is a co-founder of Hofheimer/Ferrebee, P.C., a six lawyer law firm dedicated to representing women only in divorce and custody matters.

Charlie has been married forty-two years to nationally recognized child advocate and paralegal Diane Wilson Hofheimer. Together, Charlie and Diane have been featured in an award winning documentary "Small Justice" created as a result of Diane's relentlesss commitment to children in difficult child sexual-abuse custody cases. "Small Justice" was produced in 2005 by Boston University Professor Garland Waller.

Charles and Diane have three children, a daughter-in-law, and three grandchildren, all of whom reside in Virginia.

For more information about Mr. Hofheimer or the Hofheimer/Ferrebee law firm, visit:

www.virginiadivorceattorney.com or
www.virginiacollaborativedivorceattorney.com